Maeda J. Galinsky
Janice H. Schopler
Editors

Support Groups:
Current Perspectives
on Theory and Practice

Pre-Publication
REVIEWS,
COMMENTARIES,
EVALUATIONS . . .

"**S**chopler and Galinsky reward us with a fine collection of materials dealing with a topic they have experienced first hand, investigated theoretically, and have contributed to social work's literature–*support groups.* Their conceptual contribution to work with groups, already substantial, is heightened by this carefully crafted volume which could easily be a text. The leading edge composition of chapters, engagingly described, offers experiences and ideas for group practice that will appeal to novices and seasoned practitioners alike. Additionally, there is a research component that will probably become increasingly necessary in group services. Know-how in each realm is illustrated."

Ruth R. Middleman, EdD, MSW
Professor Emerita
Kent School of Social Work
University of Louisville

"**G**alinsky and Schopler edit a highly informative special issue on the subject of support groups. Their introductory chapter superbly sets the stage for the volume. The contributors significantly enhance our knowledge base through insightful theoretical and empirical discussion and innovative practice illustrations of support groups at work."

Alex Gitterman, EdD
Professor
Columbia School of Social Work

"**T**his book is an extremely effective and practical guide to understanding the broad spectrum of groups that have been labeled "support groups." The book is grounded in theory but also presents sufficient practical examples so that students and practitioners alike can have explicit examples to follow. The fact that all the chapters follow the conceptual framework of the opem systems model assists in the clarity of presentation and in comparing the various support groups described. Galinsky and Schopler have complied a wide spectrum of support groups to illustrate their open systems concepts. Certain chapters are noteworthy for their usefulness as classroom examples–such as the study of community-based cancer support groups and support groups for women with postpartum psychiatric illness. I found this book to have the necessary but rarely found combination of theory and practical examples to satisfy the needs of the classroom. I would also say that practitioners in the field who have been hesitant to do groupwork would find this book to be a great stimulus to beginning their own groups."

Karen Subramanian, PhD
Associate Professor
USC School of Social Work

"**T**he book makes a valuable contribution to the social work literature, in that it provides the reader with a new conceptualization for viewing groups on a continuum around the organizing construct of "support." Within this framework the concept of "support groups" is the key to understanding, analyzing and intervening with groups despite the vast variations in their purpose, structure, composition, goals and outcomes. Whilst the articles most adequately serve the purpose of illustrating how this framework is applicable to a range of groups; the unique quintessence of the book lies in the excellent introductory chapter which succinctly explicates a comprehensive model for social group work which is not so clearly and concisely conceptualized in the group work literature.

Support Groups provides the blueprint for a framework of analysis, which attemps to unite the disparate and vast field of social group work."

Nazneen S. Mayadas, DSW ACSW, LMSW-ACP
Professor of Social Work
School of Social Work
University of Texas at Arlington

"**T**his book presents the reader with an excellent understanding of the current use of support groups and how this service may benefit people with many types of concerns. The volume begins with a clear and concise analysis by Galinsky and Schopler in which support groups are defined and the types of purposes such groups may fulfill is explained. This includes material on the role of the practitioner.

Our society is a highly stressful one and causes many type of problems for people who will not use or may not need psychotherapy. Support groups, as reported in the research evidence of effectiveness included in this volume are a viable service for such individuals. As this message is disseminated, practitioners are likely to use the models portrayed in this book to creatively add to the kinds of support groups that exist as well as discover even better means of facilitating such groups. Galinsky and Schopler have done a great deal in this volume, as well as in their earlier work, to make this happen."

Charles Garvin, PhD
Professor of Social Work
The School of Social Work
The University of Michigan

The Haworth Press, Inc.

Support Groups:
Current Perspectives
on Theory and Practice

The *Social Work with Groups* series:

For information on previous issues of the *Social Work with Groups* series, edited by Catherine P. Papell and Beulah Rothman, please contact: The Haworth Press, Inc., 10 Alice Street, Binghamton, NY 13904-1580 USA.

Support Groups:
Current Perspectives
on Theory and Practice

Maeda J. Galinsky, PhD
Janice H. Schopler, PhD
Editors

Routledge
Taylor & Francis Group

LONDON AND NEW YORK

First published 1995 by The Haworth Press, Inc.

2 Park Square, Milton Park, Abingdon, Oxon OX14 4RN
711 Third Avenue, New York, NY 10017, USA

Routledge is an imprint of the Taylor & Francis Group, an informa business

First issued in paperback 2016

Support Groups: Current Perspectives on Theory and Practice has also been published as *Social Work with Groups*, Volume 18, Number 1 1995.

Library of Congress Cataloging-in-Publication Data

Support groups : current perspectives on theory and practice / Maeda J. Galinsky, Janice H. Schopler, editors.
      p. cm.
      "Has also been published as Social work with groups, volume 18, number 1, 1995"–T.p. verso.
      Includes bibliographical references and index.
      1. Social group work–United States. 2. Self-help groups–United States. I. Galinsky, Maeda J. II. Schopler, Janice H.
HV45.S896 1995   95-44465
361.4–dc20   CIP

ISBN 13: 978-1-56024-763-0 (hbk)
ISBN 13: 978-1-138-98339-7 (pbk)

INDEXING & ABSTRACTING

Contributions to this publication are selectively indexed or abstracted in print, electronic, online, or CD-ROM version(s) of the reference tools and information services listed below. This list is current as of the copyright date of this publication. See the end of this section for additional notes.

- *Applied Social Sciences Index & Abstracts (ASSIA) (online: ASSI via Data-Star) (CDRom: ASSIA Plus),* Bowker-Saur Limited, Maypole House, Maypole Road, East Grinstead, West Sussex RH19 1HH, England

- *caredata CD: the social and community care database,* National Institute for Social Work, 5 Tavistock Place, London WC1H 9SS, England

- *Current Contents:* . . . see: Institute for Scientific Information

- *Guide to Social Science & Religion in Periodical Literature,* National Periodical Library, P.O. Box 3278, Clearwater, FL 34630

- *Index to Periodical Articles Related to Law,* University of Texas, 727 East 26th Street, Austin, TX 78705

- *Institute for Scientific Information,* 3501 Market Street, Philadelphia, PA 19104. Coverage in:
    a) Social Science Citation Index (SSCI): print, online, CD-ROM
    b) Research Alert (current awareness service)
    c) Social SciSearch (magnetic tape)
    d) Current Contents/Social & Behavioral Sciences (weekly current awareness service)

- *International Bulletin of Bibliography on Education,* Proyecto B.I.B.E./Apartado 52, San Lorenzo del Escorial, Madrid, Spain

(continued)

- *INTERNET ACCESS (& additional networks) Bulletin Board for Libraries ("BUBL"), coverage of information resources on INTERNET, JANET, and other networks.*
  - JANET X.29: UK.AC.BATH.BUBL or 00006012101300
  - TELNET: BUBL.BATH.AC.UK or 138.38.32.45 login 'bubl'
  - Gopher: BUBL.BATH.AC.UK (138.32.32.45). Port 7070
  - World Wide Web: http: / / www.bubl.bath.ac.uk./BUBL/ home.html
  - NISSWAIS: telnetniss.ac.uk (for the NISS gateway)
  The Andersonian Library, Curran Building, 101 St. James Road, Glasgow G4 ONS, Scotland

- *Inventory of Marriage and Family Literature (online and hard copy),* Peters Technology Transfer, 306 East Baltimore Pike, Second Floor, Media PA 19063

- *Psychological Abstracts (PsycINFO),* American Psychological Association, P.O. Box 91600, Washington, DC 20090-1600

- *Social Planning/Policy & Development Abstracts (SOPODA),* Sociological Abstracts, Inc., P.O. Box 22206, San Diego, CA 92192-0206

- *Social Work Abstracts,* National Association of Social Workers, 750 First Street NW, 8th Floor, Washington, DC 20002

- *Sociological Abstracts (SA),* Sociological Abstracts, Inc., P.O. Box 22206, San Diego, CA 92192-0206

- *Special Educational Needs Abstracts,* Carfax Information Systems, P.O. Box 25, Abingdon, Oxfordshire OX14 3UE, United Kingdom

- *Studies on Women Abstracts,* Carfax Publishing Company, P.O. Box 25, Abingdon, Oxfordshire OX14 3UE, United Kingdom

- *Violence and Abuse Abstracts: A Review of Current Literature on Interpersonal Violence (VAA),* Sage Publications, Inc., 2455 Teller Road, Newbury Park, CA 91320

SPECIAL BIBLIOGRAPHIC NOTES

related to special journal issues (separates)
and indexing/abstracting

☐ indexing/abstracting services in this list will also cover material in any "separate" that is co-published simultaneously with Haworth's special thematic journal issue or DocuSerial. Indexing/abstracting usually covers material at the article/chapter level.

☐ monographic co-editions are intended for either non-subscribers or libraries which intend to purchase a second copy for their circulating collections.

☐ monographic co-editions are reported to all jobbers/wholesalers/approval plans. The source journal is listed as the "series" to assist the prevention of duplicate purchasing in the same manner utilized for books-in-series.

☐ to facilitate user/access services all indexing/abstracting services are encouraged to utilize the co-indexing entry note indicated at the bottom of the first page of each article/chapter/contribution.

☐ this is intended to assist a library user of any reference tool (whether print, electronic, online, or CD-ROM) to locate the monographic version if the library has purchased this version but not a subscription to the source journal.

☐ individual articles/chapters in any Haworth publication are also available through the Haworth Document Delivery Services (HDDS).

Support Groups:
Current Perspectives
on Theory and Practice

CONTENTS

ABOUT THE EDITOR

Maeda J. Galinsky, PhD, is William R. Kenan, Jr., Professor of the School of Social Work at the University of North Carolina at Chapel Hill. She has over 30 years of experience teaching at the university level, with her areas of expertise in group work theory and practice, evaluation of group work practice, theoretical bases of micro level practice, and institutional discrimination. Her current research projects include an evaluation of telephone support groups for persons with HIV and differences in leadership of telephone groups and face-to-face groups. Widely published in books and journals, Dr. Galinsky is co-author of "Group Practice: Theory and Evaluation" in the 19th edition (1995) of *The Encyclopedia of Social Work.*

Janice H. Schopler, PhD, is Professor and Associate Dean of the School of Social Work at the University of North Carolina at Chapel Hill. She teaches in the areas of social group work, macro social work practice, and services to families and children. Her writing and research have focused on the development and testing of social intervention theory, particularly in the area of group practice, and on conceptualizing and evaluating interorganizational systems. Author or co-author of books, book chapters, and articles, Dr. Schopler is co-author of "Group Practice: Theory and Evaluation" in the 19th edition (1995) of *The Encyclopedia of Social Work.*

FROM THE EDITORS

This volume is a special one about support groups edited by Maeda J. Galinsky and Janice H. Schopler, who have studied and written about support groups and their use to respond to the needs of people addressing crises, life transitions, and chronic conditions. The use of support groups in the field is growing. This volume aims to expand the theoretical and empirical base for understanding them as well as to report on their innovative use in a range of settings and with diverse populations.

Roselle Kurland
Andrew Malekoff
Editors

[Haworth co-indexing entry note]: "From the Editors." Kurland, Roselle, and Andrew Malekoff. Co-published simultaneously in *Social Work with Groups* (The Haworth Press, Inc.) Vol. 18, No. 1, 1995, p. 1; and: *Support Groups: Current Perspectives on Theory and Practice* (ed: Maeda J. Galinsky, and Janice H. Schopler) The Haworth Press, Inc., 1995, p. 1. Single or multiple copies of this article are available from The Haworth Document Delivery Center [1-800-342-9678, 9:00 a.m. - 5:00 p.m. (EST)].

Expanding Our View of Support Groups as Open Systems

Janice H. Schopler
Maeda J. Galinsky

SUMMARY. The open systems model of support groups (Schopler & Galinsky, 1993) provides the organizing concepts for the articles in this volume. Support groups are conceived as the center of a continuum of supportive group interventions, overlapping with self-help groups at one end and treatment groups at the other. The open systems model of support groups is a framework for understanding the factors that affect support groups, for guiding interventions, and for evaluating their outcomes. The major conceptual dimensions addressed by the model are environmental conditions, participant characteristics, group conditions, and outcomes. An overview of major concepts is followed by a discussion of the contribution of each of the articles to an expanded view of support groups. *[Single or multiple copies of this article are available from The Haworth Document Delivery Service: 1-800-342-9678, 9:00 a.m. - 5:00 p.m. (EST).]*

This volume has evolved from our continuing study of support groups and the ways they are used to respond to the needs of people dealing with crises, life transitions, and chronic conditions (Schopler & Galinsky, 1993; Galinsky & Schopler, 1994). Our interest in

Janice H. Schopler, PhD, is Professor and Associate Dean and Maeda J. Galinsky, PhD, is William R. Kenan, Jr. Professor at The University of North Carolina School of Social Work, 223 East Franklin Street, CB #3550, Chapel Hill, NC 27599-3550.

[Haworth co-indexing entry note]: "Expanding Our View of Support Groups as Open Systems." Schopler, Janice H., and Maeda J. Galinsky. Co-published simultaneously in *Social Work with Groups* (The Haworth Press, Inc.) Vol. 18, No. 1, 1995, pp. 3-10; and: *Support Groups: Current Perspectives on Theory and Practice* (ed: Maeda J. Galinsky, and Janice H. Schopler) The Haworth Press, Inc., 1995, pp. 3-10. Single or multiple copies of this article are available from The Haworth Document Delivery Center [1-800-342-9678, 9:00 a.m. - 5:00 p.m. (EST)].

support groups stems from the recognition that these groups can be an important source of emotional support, guidance, and information for people who are dealing with common sources of stress, and our concern that theory and research have not kept pace with practice. This volume expands the theoretical and empirical base for understanding support groups and reports on innovative practice.

CONTINUUM OF SUPPORTIVE GROUP INTERVENTIONS

Supportive group interventions come in many group forms, labeled variously as self-help, mutual help, mutual assistance, treatment, and support. While the particular label may be irrelevant, understanding the distinctions among the various group forms can be important to practitioners and researchers. Practitioners need to know which type of group characteristics will be most responsive to a particular client's needs. Researchers need to know the characteristics of the groups they are evaluating and comparing to reach valid conclusions. The central differences among the various forms of supportive group interventions relate to sponsorship, conceptions of participant roles, the basis of leadership, interventive methods and technology, and the view of the group. Our main focus in this volume is on those groups which we have labeled as support groups.

Support groups can be conceptualized as the center of a continuum of these supportive group interventions, overlapping with self-help groups at one end and treatment groups at the other (Schopler & Galinsky, 1993). Support groups are distinguished by the following characteristics. They may have organizational sponsorship or be the creation of an innovative practitioner. Some support groups are associated with national organizations; others are created by local practitioners. Support groups are member-centered; leadership is provided by professionals, volunteers, or, at times, by members. Although leaders share authority and are on somewhat equal terms with members, their legitimacy tends to be based on training and expertise as group facilitators. Frequently, leaders have personal experience with the group's focal concern such as breast cancer, parenting adolescents, or unemployment; but, this is not required for leadership of support groups as it often is for self-help groups. As Schwartz (1961, 1971) advocates in his concept of "mutual aid," the support group leader's task is to promote the development of helping relationships among members. Members usually are expected to share their experiences, provide information, give advice, and draw out other members. The intervention technology of support groups tends to be varied, ranging from open discussion to more structured sessions that engage members in developing understanding, skill development, and problem-solving. The group provides a supportive environment and a means for developing coping abilities, but typically does not have an advocacy function.

OPEN SYSTEMS MODEL OF SUPPORT GROUPS

The open systems model of support groups is a framework for understanding the factors that affect support groups, for guiding interventions, and for evaluating their outcomes. (For a full discussion of the model, see Schopler & Galinsky, 1993). The major conceptual dimensions addressed by the model are environmental conditions, participant characteristics, group conditions, and outcomes. The following brief description of each of the conceptual dimensions provides the basis for understanding support groups as open systems.

Environmental Conditions. Environmental resources and constraints affect the initial formation of support groups and their development over time. Critical resources important to support groups include a pool of potential members, a sponsoring organization or individual to provide a meeting place and facilitate collaborative arrangements, funding, staff and volunteers to implement group activities, and other support systems available to potential members. Factors that constrain group activity and outcomes include screening procedures, transportation, institutional barriers, conflicting organizational priorities, and other demands on potential participants' time.

Participant Characteristics. Group activities and group development over time are directly influenced by the characteristics of the group participants, both the members and the leaders. Although the importance of specific characteristics varies with the purpose of the group, the way the group evolves and what it will accomplish are shaped by the size of the group, the specific composition, and the intervention technology. The *size and composition* vary widely, from groups with a stable, predetermined membership and leadership to groups with constantly changing members and leaders. Whether the leadership is provided by professionals, volunteers, or members, the *intervention technology* used in the group is based on the knowledge and experience of the leaders and their level of skill and particular interventive approach.

Group Conditions. Successful support groups must organize their work to pursue common goals and develop a structure that is flexible enough to adapt to changing conditions over time. The goals, structural form, and developmental patterns of the support group system mediate the impact of both environmental conditions and participant characteristics and directly influence group outcomes. Whether similar or different, the *goals* and expectations of the members, leaders, and constituents (e.g., organizational sponsor, relatives) all merit attention. Typical goals include emotional release, validation of concerns, reduction of social isolation, information, improved coping, decreased stress, problem-solving, and, at times, advocacy. *Structure* can be described in terms of roles and bonds, norms and culture, group operating procedures, and meeting format. When membership is open, members may have less opportunity to develop strong bonds and the leader may assume major responsibility for facilitating group interaction to assure continuity. In more stable groups, responsibility is more likely to be shared with members who may assume many of the leadership tasks. The norms and culture that develop in relation to issues, such as attendance, self-disclosure, participation, and confidentiality, affect member investment in the group, adherence to group rules, and member satisfaction. The format of support group meetings varies extensively, from unstructured discussion to highly structured activities and use of multi-media technology. *Group development* varies with the continuity of membership and duration of the group.

Outcomes. Support group interventions can result in a range of outcomes, including positive effects, negative effects, group problems, and ethical and legal issues. While any evaluation of support group success should consider all potential outcomes, the positive effects for members, including greater social resources, increased knowledge about the focal concern, a sense of relief and reassur-

ance, and enhanced skills for coping, have received the most attention in the literature. Organizational benefits, such as leader satisfaction and more responsive, cost-effective service delivery, are
also mentioned. Because the literature tends to report only successful group experiences, outcomes such as negative effects for members and organizations, group problems, and ethical and legal issues
are seldom considered.

Our literature review and pilot research suggest that supportive
interventions do not always have positive outcomes and negative
effects may be as critical to consider as the benefits (Galinsky &
Schopler, 1994). Supportive interventions can result in such negative effects for members as pressure to conform, stress related to
group obligations, feeling overwhelmed and less adequate, learning
ineffective and inappropriate responses, embarrassment, and over-
confidence. Leaders can suffer from burnout and interdisciplinary
tensions. When groups fail, they can detract from the organizational
image. Questions about confidentiality and destructive behaviors
raise legal and ethical issues.

UNDERSTANDING SUPPORT GROUPS
THROUGH RESEARCH AND PRACTICE

The contributions of practitioners, educators and researchers to
this volume have enriched our understanding of the support group
experience. The articles expand our knowledge about the range of
supportive group interventions and the content of the groups. They
also provide data about the current status of support groups and
describe exciting practice innovations.

The review of the practice and research literature related to supportive group interventions for caregivers of frail older adults by
McCallion and Toseland provides a comprehensive overview of the
kinds of services that are now offered to this population and the
outcomes achieved. They enlarge our understanding of what a full
range of group services can look like when practitioners and con-
sumers respond to the needs of particular populations. Their conceptualization of support groups adds social and recreational groups
to the support group continuum, reconnecting us to our roots in

settlement houses and community centers where such groups were an important part of practice.

Glajchen and Magen report on their study of process and outcomes in community-based cancer support groups designed for patients, relatives and bereaved spouses and led by trained social work practitioners. They link practice in these prototypical support groups with both theory and research and illustrate how the collection of systematic data in an ongoing program can add to the advancement of knowledge about support group practice. Further, their study confirms the feasibility of conducting research in an ongoing program of services and of collaboration between agency and academia.

Fairchild's article about women with postpartum psychiatric illness represents the treatment end of the continuum of supportive group interventions. She makes a convincing case for having a facilitator who has the expertise to address important treatment issues that must be resolved in order for members of this population to feel supported. This article demonstrates the overlap of support groups with treatment groups and justifies the need for professional leadership for especially vulnerable populations.

Kramer and Nash apply ecological theory to an understanding of findings from their nationwide sample of groups for African-Americans affected by sickle cell disease. Their research findings reinforce the importance of conducting systematic surveys of group characteristics to develop knowledge about supportive group interventions. The groups they describe occupy a position toward the self-help end of the continuum of supportive group interventions. They alert us to the interplay between self-help and support groups and discuss how diverse forms of group development are related to the ever-changing features of the environment.

Cohen's article portrays an organizational response to needs expressed by a client population, grandmothers raising their children's children. She stresses the importance of the organizational context and organizational factors in effective support group implementation, emphasizing the environmental conditions as well as participant characteristics. Cohen also alerts us to the necessity of providing workers who lead groups with adequate training and continuing supervision.

The next two articles describe support group practice with populations recently identified as needing supportive interventions. Reid, Mathews and Liss describe group work with male partners of adult survivors of sexual abuse and give ample testimony of why support groups are needed for this overlooked population. They examine a group program developed in a community agency and pay particular attention to the sequencing of groups for these "secondary victims," to the inclusion of male survivors in such groups, and to issues of mixed gender leadership. Parker, Hutchinson and Berry elaborate on an interorganizational support group for military dependents in crisis. Their article describes the way in which two diverse agencies collaborated to provide supportive group services for whole families who were greatly affected when a member was called to serve in the Middle East during the recent Persian Gulf War and the kinds of group processes and activities that occurred in this multi-family, multi-generational group.

The last two articles in this volume explore the growing use of technology in group work practice. Meier, Galinsky and Rounds discuss how telephone conference calls can be used to offer support groups to caregivers of persons with AIDS. They note how a telephone support group can meet the needs of this population, often homebound and frequently stigmatized, and present the major objectives and themes of a semi-structured eight session protocol to address these needs. Finn's article considers how the computer can be used as an adjunct to support groups. He examines the advantages of utilizing computer-based groups to supplement face-to-face groups and describes a pilot project which utilizes a computer-based self-help group as a resource for group members who are survivors of sexual abuse.

These nine articles enlarge our perspective on support groups and deepen our understanding of factors that have an impact on the formation and implementation of supportive group interventions. They add to the information that we have on environmental conditions, participant characteristics, group conditions and outcomes in current support group practice. Further, they point to the responsive and innovative support group practice that has evolved in the world of practice and they draw attention to the need for further theoretical development and research.

REFERENCES

Galinsky, M.J., & Schopler, J.H. (1994). Negative experiences in support groups. *Social Work in Health Care, 20* (1), 77-95.

Schopler, J.H., & Galinsky, M.J. (1993, August). Support groups as open systems: A model for practice and research. *Health & Social Work, 18,* 195-207.

Schwartz, W. (1961). The social worker in the group. In *The Social Welfare Forum* (pp. 146-174). New York: Columbia University Press.

Schwartz, W. (1971). Social group work: The interactionist approach. In R. Morris (Ed.), *Encyclopedia of social work* (16th ed., Vol. 2, pp. 1252-1263). New York: National Association of Social Workers.

Supportive Group Interventions with Caregivers of Frail Older Adults

Philip McCallion
Ronald W. Toseland

SUMMARY. The use of supportive group interventions with caregivers of frail older adults is discussed in this article. Four categories of group interventions are described: (1) mutual support groups, (2) psychoeducational groups, (3) social, recreational and educational groups, and (4) service and advocacy groups. Research evidence on the efficacy of group interventions with this population is also considered. Recommendations are made on when to refer caregivers to support groups and on what type of support group is most appropriate. Consideration by practitioners and program planners of a broader range of types of supportive groups is also encouraged. *[Single or multiple copies of this article are available from The Haworth Document Delivery Service: 1-800-342-9678, 9:00 a.m. - 5:00 p.m. (EST).]*

In a recent article, Schopler and Galinsky (1993) outline an open systems model to guide the development of research and practice with support groups. They recommend that additional research is needed to elaborate the model, determine how it applies to different

Philip McCallion, PhD, is Research Associate, Ringel Institute of Gerontology, University at Albany, State University of New York, Albany, NY 12222. Ronald W. Toseland, PhD, is Director, Ringel Institute of Gerontology, and Professor, School of Social Welfare, University at Albany, State University of New York, Albany, NY 12222.

[Haworth co-indexing entry note]: "Supportive Group Interventions with Caregivers of Frail Older Adults." McCallion, Philip, and Ronald W. Toseland. Co-published simultaneously in *Social Work with Groups* (The Haworth Press, Inc.) Vol. 18, No. 1, 1995, pp. 11-25; and: *Support Groups: Current Perspectives on Theory and Practice* (ed: Maeda J. Galinsky, and Janice H. Schopler) The Haworth Press, Inc., 1995, pp. 11-25. Single or multiple copies of this article are available from The Haworth Document Delivery Center [1-800-342-9678, 9:00 a.m. - 5:00 p.m. (EST)].

11

populations and consider how it distinguishes between different types of groups. In keeping with these recommendations, this article describes one population to which the open systems model for support group interventions may be applied, family caregivers of frail elderly persons. It contributes to the enhancement of the open systems model by describing different types of supportive group interventions that can be used to meet the diverse needs of caregivers.

FRAIL OLDER PERSONS AND THEIR INFORMAL CAREGIVERS

In recent years, there has been growing recognition that the elderly represent an increasing proportion of the population and that their health care and residential needs will pose a growing demand on available resources (Gevalnik & Simonsick, 1993; Schneider & Guralnik, 1990). Most elderly persons in need of long-term care receive informal support from family and friends (Doty, 1986). Moreover, having a spouse or adult child caregiver reduces the risk of institutionalization (Pearlman & Crown, 1992). Thus, informal caregivers provide essential support for frail older adults that would otherwise have to be provided by an already strained formal care system. Primary informal caregivers are usually female, and most often a spouse. If a spouse is not available, an adult daughter, an adult son, or other relatives such as daughters-in-law, the care recipient's siblings, granddaughters, or friends provide care (Tonti, 1988).

There is evidence that caregiving is often experienced as a rewarding and fulfilling experience (Lawton, Kleban, Moss, Rovine, & Glicksman, 1989). Yet, caregiving may also cause a variety of physical, psychological, and social problems. Physical problems include sleeplessness, fatigue, back problems, and other somatic complaints. Psychological problems include depression, guilt and uncertainty, conflicts with other family members over caregiving responsibilities, and a general sense of anxiety and worry. Social problems include growing isolation, caregivers denying their own needs for contacts with friends and family, and conflict between work, child care responsibilities, and caregiving for frail elders (see Toseland & Rossiter, 1989; Toseland, Smith, & McCallion, in press, for a more complete discussion of the physical, psychological and social problems experienced by caregivers of the frail elderly).

SUPPORTIVE GROUP WORK WITH CAREGIVERS

Caregivers are a very heterogenous group with a broad range of needs. Four categories of supportive group interventions that can meet the broad range of needs manifested by caregivers include: (1) mutual support groups, (2) psychoeducational groups, (3) social, recreational and educational groups, and (4) service and advocacy groups. The supportive characteristics of each of these types of groups are described in the following sections.

MUTUAL SUPPORT GROUPS

Mutual support groups are designed to help caregivers cope with the stresses of caregiving and to sustain and enhance their coping abilities. In mutual support groups, psychological closeness is encouraged by the knowledge that members share similar concerns that are often not well understood by others. Mutual support group members offer understanding, information, and mutual aid. They also serve as a resource for social contacts. They help caregivers to overcome isolation and expand their informal support networks. Weiss (1974) lists six different functions of social relationships which he perceives as the "main ingredients" of interpersonal support: attachment, social integration, opportunity for nurturance, reassurance of worth, a sense of reliable alliance, and the obtaining of guidance. These six functions are at the core of most caregiver mutual support groups.

Meetings of caregiver mutual support groups are characterized by back and forth interaction among members. Members participate at their own pace, revitalizing, adjusting, and enhancing coping capacities that they have developed over a lifetime. During the sessions, members are encouraged to listen empathetically, to support each other, to give and receive advice about effective coping strategies, and to provide each other with hope. Members become peer models of effective coping, enabling each other to take the necessary steps to sustain and enhance their own coping capacities. Each caregiver also has the opportunity to demonstrate his or her own wisdom and experience and to play a useful and meaningful role in helping others.

There is often a high level of social interaction among members of mutual support groups that may be unrelated to the group's central concerns, for example, exchanging photographs and anecdotes about grandchildren. This interaction is important too, because it helps establish social networks among members that are often relied upon between group meetings and after the group has terminated.

Mutual support groups have several characteristic features that tend to distinguish them from other supportive group interventions. They are frequently facilitated by lay persons who have experience as caregivers, rather than by professionals. Often, they are ongoing, long-term groups, providing caregivers with a resource they can rely on over a "career" of caregiving that may last for many years. Although some mutual support groups decide to close their membership so that the group can grow and develop intimacy, frequently, participants can enter and leave as they wish in a flexible manner that meets the needs of their personal caregiving situation.

PSYCHOEDUCATIONAL GROUPS

While the goal of mutual support groups is to help high functioning caregivers cope with stressful caregiving situations, the goal of psychoeducational groups is to help caregivers who are experiencing problems in coping with stressful caregiving situations. These problems may be related to the stressful caregiving situation alone, but are often exacerbated by other long standing problems. Psychoeducational groups can help by: (1) increasing caregivers' understanding of the relative for whom they are caring, (2) enabling caregivers to make better use of informal and formal supports, (3) improving caregivers' coping abilities, (4) encouraging caregivers to take better care of themselves by balancing the needs of others with their own needs, (5) improving problematic relationships with the care recipient or other family members, and (6) improving caregivers' home care and behavior-management skills (McCallion, Toseland, and Diehl, 1993).

Psychoeducational groups are particularly helpful for adult children caregivers who are experiencing family conflict. There appears to be a direct relationship between family conflict and mental health problems (Strawbridge & Wallhagan, 1991). For example, psychological problems are more likely to occur among adult children who are caregivers, when they are already experiencing marital conflict, when they argue with their mates about the care of a parent or parent-in-law, or when their own children resent the time they spend caring for their parent. There is also evidence that some adult daughter caregivers resent siblings who do not assist with care and become distressed by siblings who criticize them or who fail to give emotional or instrumental support (Brody et al., 1989). Longstanding family conflicts may also have an impact. Daughters may revisit old conflicts with the parent now in need of care, or with siblings with whom they have not gotten along for years (Gatz, Benngtson, & Blum, 1990; Tonti, 1988). Not only do these factors increase stress for the caregiver, but the caregiver is often loathe to discuss them openly with other family members and tends to avoid conflict by not seeking help and becoming more isolated.

Psychoeducational groups can also be helpful resources for caregiving spouses, especially those who are experiencing problems but resist help. Caregiving spouses tend to be older and in poor health themselves, and typically provide care for longer periods, in more physically demanding situations, and with fewer supports than other types of family caregivers (Montgomery & Datwyler, 1990). Yet, it has been found that caregiving spouses often do not ask other family members for appropriate help and are resistant to the idea of institutionalizing their husband or wife (Montgomery & Kosloski, 1994). This creates family tension, further reduces the level of support available from other family members, makes care more burdensome and demanding, and possibly precipitates the crisis spouse caregivers wish to avoid (Townsend & Noelker, 1987).

Even when members of a psychoeducational group share many similarities in their caregiving and family experiences, their problems often have unique aspects. Therefore, psychoeducational group meetings are frequently characterized by a focus on the concerns of individual members who take turns receiving assistance from the group. For this approach to be effective for all the group members, the leader must ensure that the dyadic interaction between the individual caregiver and the leader also benefits the other members.

Many different approaches can be used to facilitate psychoeducational groups depending on the theoretical orientation of the leader and the needs and preferences of members. However, one widely used approach that is compatible with a number of different theoretical orientations is problem solving. An eight step model has been found to be effective (see, for example, Toseland, Rossiter, & Labrecque, 1989a).

Step 1; Identifying each caregiver's problem.

Step 2; Data gathering focused on the antecedents and consequences of the problem.

Step 3; Generating alternative solutions by all members of the group while suspending any evaluation of the value of the solutions.

Step 4; Examining the advantages and disadvantages of each solution.

Step 5; Developing an action plan.

Step 6; Anticipating any obstacles to plan implementation, and rehearsing the plan.

Step 7; Carrying out the plan.

Step 8; Evaluating and modifying the plan as necessary.

The steps in the problem-solving approach lend themselves to helping members focus upon their specific problems. Yet, the approach also helps all members to participate actively by giving suggestions based upon their own experiences and successes and by gaining ideas that may be useful in their own situation.

Psychoeducational groups are characterized by an expectation of a high level of self-disclosure. In order to encourage the development of intimacy, and feelings of safety and comfort necessary for a high level of self-disclosure, psychoeducational groups are frequently closed to new members. Also, they are more likely than mutual support groups to focus on specific goals, and to use structured, short-term approaches with specific agendas for each meeting. Because of the specialized knowledge necessary to lead such groups, and the nature of the problems experienced by members, psychoeducational groups for caregivers are almost always facilitated by professionals rather than by peers.

SOCIAL, RECREATIONAL, AND EDUCATIONAL GROUPS

Social, recreational and educational groups enable caregivers to meet their needs for social contact, recreation, self-enrichment, and fun. Of all the kinds of social support available to caregivers of the frail elderly, some evidence suggests that the most important is the opportunity to socialize and be engaged with friends, family and acquaintances. For example, in one study of 217 family caregivers of frail elders, as the care recipient's dependency increased, caregivers who lacked opportunities for fun, recreation and social participation were more likely to experience increased stress than caregivers who had these opportunities (Thompson, Futterman, Gallagher-Thompson, Rose, & Lovett, 1993). Social, recreational, and educational groups can help to meet these caregiver needs.

Social, recreational, and educational groups share several features that separate them from other types of supportive group interventions for caregivers. The first feature is that they emphasize primary prevention (Toseland, 1995). Social, recreational, and educational groups maintain and enhance caregivers' abilities. As caregivers engage in activities and learn new information and skills, they acknowledge, affirm, and validate each other's abilities. This, in turn, helps caregivers to feel useful and competent, improving self-esteem, self-worth, and self-confidence.

The second distinguishing feature of these groups is that they foster the development of social support, comraderie, and a spirit of community in an atmosphere and a setting that is not linked to the caregiving situation. Through the group caregivers are able to stay actively involved with friends and peers in activities that interest them. The group promotes the development of informal support networks, and helps members feel secure by providing a reference group, and a forum to maintain and enhance their own identities and personalities which they can experience in relation to others. As a result, isolation and social withdrawal can be prevented.

A third distinguishing feature of social, recreational, and educational groups is their reliance upon program activities as the medium to engage members, to promote social interaction, and to sustain interest in the group (Toseland, in press). The members' common interest in the group's social, recreational, or educational activity and the experiences they share as a result of engaging in it, form the bond among them. For this reason, unlike the groups already discussed, it is not necessary that the social, recreational, or educational group be open only to caregivers. Caregiving is not the common bond, the shared activity is. Program activities include those that are focused on: (1) discussion of current events, (2) reminiscence and life review, (3) educational topics, (4) aerobic and other physical exercise, (5) dance, theater, and other expressive activities, (6) special events, and (7) table games. Caregivers are likely to find social, recreational, and educational groups especially enjoyable when they perceive that (1) there will be benefits from participation, (2) program activities reflect their interests and motivations and are attuned to their abilities, capacities, skills and talents, (3) needed resources are readily available, and (4) both their socio-emotional needs and their needs for task accomplishment are met (Toseland, in press).

Social, recreational, and educational groups may be either short-term or long-term. Long-term groups often have to guard against members forming exclusive cliques that may not welcome new members. Social, recreational, and educational groups are usually open-membered and, depending upon their content, led by non-professionals or professionals who have specialized expertise in the particular program activities sponsored by the group.

SERVICE AND ADVOCACY GROUPS

While providing support for members, service and advocacy groups also help individuals who are not part of the group. For example, members of service groups may work as volunteers or raise funds to meet the needs of children, patients in hospitals, or homebound elderly. These activities do not carry a direct benefit for the caregivers involved, although participation often carries important indirect therapeutic benefits for them. Although service and advocacy organizations are usually open to new members, a committed core of members often develops. It is also more likely that leaders will be non-professional peers, and, in the case of service groups, may not be caregivers themselves.

Despite their primary focus on helping a larger constituency outside of the group, the benefits to caregivers of participating in service and advocacy groups should not be underestimated. Through their involvement in service and advocacy groups caregivers are able to engage in meaningful social roles. They are able to share experiences they have accumulated over a lifetime, feel good about their ability to contribute to others, and feel proud of the wisdom and experience they possess. In service groups, caregivers have an opportunity to socialize with peers while pursuing activities that interest them, and to display and use their skills and talents in a beneficial way. In advocacy groups, caregivers can regain a sense of control, empowerment, and self-efficacy in their own lives and can improve their own living situation, as well as the situations of the larger constituency the group represents. Also, the advocacy group's activities may directly benefit the caregivers involved. For example, if caregivers in an advocacy group such as a local chapter of the Alzheimer's Association successfully lobby for an extension of funding for respite services for caregiving families, they too will experience greater access to these resources.

Service and advocacy groups are more likely to be long-term rather than short-term in focus. They also tend to meet less frequently than other groups. Meetings often occur monthly, and much of the group's business can be conducted through telephone contacts, mailings, and newsletters. This makes them attractive to some caregivers who have difficulty finding alternate caretakers for the care recipient.

Compared to the other types of groups for caregivers which have been described, there is less of an emphasis on self-disclosure in service and advocacy groups. However, as members get to know one another, close friendships may form that lead to such disclosures.

EFFICACY OF CAREGIVER SUPPORT GROUPS

Almost all of the research evidence on the efficacy of support groups for caregivers focuses upon mutual support and psycho-educational groups. Several reviews of the literature suggest that mutual support and psychoeducational groups are moderately effective for reducing the physical, social, and psychological problems which can accompany caregiving (see Biegel, Sales, & Schulz, 1991; Gallagher-Thompson, 1994; McCallion, Diehl, & Toseland, 1994, McCallion et al., 1993; Toseland & Rossiter, 1989; Zarit & Teri, 1991). However, the reviews provide little guidance to practitioners and program planners confronted with questions about when to refer caregivers to support groups, and what type of support group is most appropriate. In this article we will draw upon the available research literature to address these questions.

WHEN TO REFER TO SUPPORT GROUPS

Overall, individual, group, and family interventions can all be effective in helping caregivers to cope with the stresses of caregiving. However, some research evidence suggests that individual interventions are particularly effective when caregivers' presenting problems are psychological (Toseland, Rossiter, Peak, & Smith, 1990), and family interventions are particularly effective for helping nuclear and extended families make difficult elder care decisions (Parsons & Cox, 1989; Zarit, Anthony and Boutselis, 1987). In contrast, group interventions are particularly effective when caregivers are struggling with social isolation or a lack of social support (Toseland et al., 1990). Group interventions can also be particularly effective for caregivers who are reluctant to engage in one-to-one or family counseling (McCallion et al., 1993).

WHAT TYPE OF SUPPORT GROUP

Some information is available to practitioners and program planners on the comparative effectiveness of different types of groups, particularly mutual support and psychoeducational groups. In a study comparing mutual support and psychoeducational support groups to a respite only control condition Toseland and colleagues (Toseland, Rossiter, & Labrecque, 1989b) found that mutual support groups were about as effective as psychoeducational groups for most caregivers. Indeed, mutual support groups were marginally more effective in expanding informal support networks than psychoeducational groups. Participants in mutual support groups added an average of four people to their support network, whereas participants in psychoeducational groups added an average of three new people. A review of the session tapes suggested that socializing, sharing personal experiences, and ventilating feelings, were more prevalent in mutual support groups, and this, in turn, appeared to have a positive impact upon social networking among the members (Toseland et al., 1989b). This is consistent with Gonyea and Silverstein's finding (1991) that caregivers of Alzheimer's disease patients participating in mutual support groups were more likely to use community services. Caregivers' use of community support services was positively correlated with the length of time they belonged to the mutual support group and with the number of group meetings they attended during the previous 12 months (Gonyea & Silverstein, 1991).

Toseland and his colleagues also found, however, that mutual support groups were somewhat less effective than psychoeducational groups in improving caregivers' psychological functioning. For participants in psychoeducational groups there was a greater decrease in the absolute number of symptomatic disturbances, as measured by the Brief Symptom Inventory (Derogatis & Spencer, 1982), and a greater improvement in well-being, as measured by the Bradburn Affect Balance Scale (Bradburn, 1969). These participants also showed greater improvement on measures of personal change. After analyzing the session tapes, Toseland and colleagues concluded that the professional leaders of psychoeducational groups were more structured in their approach, were more successful in keeping participants focused on caregiving issues, and were more likely to enable the formation of plans to address caregiver concerns. They also noted, however, that some caregivers were resistant to both the greater structure of the groups and the more active leadership of the professionals who conducted the groups (Toseland et al., 1989b).

Overall, the available literature suggests to practitioners and program planners that both mutual support and psychoeducational groups can be helpful for caregivers. The literature is silent on the relative effectiveness of social, recreational, educational, service, and advocacy groups. However, when caregivers express a need to socialize, to recreate, or to use their talents to help others, practitioners should seriously consider referring caregivers to these groups.

Another important issue for practitioners and program planners is whether caregiver support groups should be short-term or long-term. A number of studies have examined the effectiveness of short-term supportive group interventions for caregivers and found that modest treatment gains often occur by the time the groups end (Brahce, 1989; Gray, 1983; Greene & Monahan, 1989; Haley, Brown, & Levine, 1987; Montgomery & Borgatta, 1989; Zarit, Anthony, & Boutselis, 1987).

Clearly, however, many caregivers have long-term needs, and many community-based support groups for caregivers are long-term. Thus, there is a pressing need to consider if longer-term group interventions, or periodic group booster sessions after short-term, intensive group programs produce larger or more sustained effects. Two studies have addressed this issue. Toseland and colleagues (Labrecque, Peak, & Toseland, 1992) designed a supportive group intervention program for spouses of frail veterans which included 8 weekly group sessions followed by 10 monthly group sessions. More recently, Mittelman and colleagues (Mittelman et al., 1994) designed an intervention that for the first four months provided individual and family counseling and then encouraged the caregiver to attend weekly meetings of an on-going, open-membered, mutual support group. Both programs proved effective in helping caregivers cope. In fact, the program developed by Mittelman and colleagues reduced admissions of the care recipient to long-term care facilities, and the program developed by Toseland and colleagues significantly reduced both inpatient and outpatient health care costs incurred by the care recipient (Peak, 1993).

CONCLUSIONS

Supportive group interventions are important resources for the caregivers of frail older adults. They have the potential to help caregivers cope with their situation at relatively low cost to the larger society. There is also evidence that supportive group interventions can strengthen the support network of socially isolated caregivers, educate caregivers about community resources and alternative coping skills, and help caregivers recognize and meet their own needs.

One should keep in mind, however, that there are great inter-individual differences among caregivers. Traditionally, support groups for caregivers have been narrowly conceived as consisting of mutual support and psychoeducational interventions. This emphasis reflects a belief that problem resolution is the paramount concern. While problem resolution is an important activity, this article points out that other types of groups can provide support for caregivers. Such groups utilize the knowledge and strengths that caregivers have accumulated during the course of caregiving. They recognize caregivers' needs for pleasurable social activities and for meaningful social roles other than caregiver. They enable caregivers to socialize, to recreate, and to use their talents to help others. A broad range of supportive group interventions can best meet the needs manifested by caregivers of frail older adults.

REFERENCES

Biegel, D. E., Sales, E., & Schulz, R. (1991). *Family caregiving in chronic illness.* Newbury Park, CA: Sage.

Bradburn, N. (1969). *The structure of psychological well-being.* Chicago: Aldine.

Brahce, C.I. (1989). The effect of a support and education program on stress and burden among family caregivers to frail elderly persons. *The Gerontologist, 29,* 472-477.

Brody, E.M., Hoffman, C., Kleban, M.H., & Schoonover, C.B. (1989). Caregiving daughters and their local siblings: Perceptions, strains, and interactions. *The Gerontologist, 29,* 529-538.

Derogatis, L., & Spencer, P. (1982). *Administration and procedures: Brief Symptom Inventory Manual.* Baltimore, MD: John Hopkins University Press.

Doty, P. (1986). Family care of the elderly: The role of public policy. *The Milbank Quarterly, 67,* 485-506.

Gallagher-Thompson, D. (1994). Clinical intervention strategies for distressed caregivers: Rationale and development of psychoeducational approaches. In E. Light, G. Niederehe, & B.D. Lebowitz (Eds.). *Stress effects on family caregivers of Alzheimer's patients* (261-277). New York: Springer.

Gatz, M., Benngtson, V.L., & Blum, M.J. (1990). Caregiving families. In J.E. Birren, & K.W. Schaie (Eds.). *Handbook of the psychology of aging.* (3rd Edition). San Diego, CA: Academic Press.

Gevalnik, J.M., & Simonsick, E.M. (1993). Physical disability in older Americans. *The Journals of Gerontology, 48* (Special Issue), 3-10.

Gonyea, J.G., & Silverstein, N.M. (1991). The role of Alzheimer's disease support groups in families' utilization of community services. *Journal of Gerontological Social Work, 16,* 43-55.

Gray, V.K. (1983). Providing support for home caregivers. In M.A. Smyer & M. Gatz (Eds.), *Mental Health and Aging* (pp. 197-214). Beverly Hills, CA: Sage.

Greene, V.L., & Monahan, D.J. (1989). The effect of a support and education program on stress and burden among family caregivers to frail elderly persons. *The Gerontologist, 29,* 471-477.

Haley, W., Brown, L., & Levine, E. (1987). Experimental evaluation of the effectiveness of group interventions for dementia caregivers. *The Gerontologist, 27,* 376-382.

Labrecque, M., Peak, T., & Toseland, R.W. (1992). The long-term effectiveness of a group program for caregivers of frail elderly veterans. *International Journal of Orthopsychiatry, 62,* 575-588.

Lawton, M.P., Brody, E.M., & Saperstein, A.R. (1989). A controlled study of respite services for caregivers of Alzheimer's patients. *The Gerontologist, 29,* 8-16.

Lawton, M.P., Kleban, M.H., Moss, M., Rovine, M., & Glicksman, A., (1989). Measuring caregiver appraisal. *Journal of Gerontology, 44,* 61-71.

McCallion, P., Diehl, M., & Toseland, R. (1994). Support group intervention for family caregivers of Alzheimer's Disease patients. *Seminars in Speech and Language, 15,* 257-270.

McCallion, P., Toseland, R.W., & Diehl, M. (1993). Social work practice with caregivers of frail older adults. *Research in Social Work Practice, 4,* 64-88.

Mittelman, M., Ferris, S., Shulman, E., Steinberg, G., Mackell, J., & Ambinder, A. (1994). Efficacy of multicomponent individualized treatment to improve the well-being of Alzheimer's caregivers. In E. Light, G. Niederehe, & B.D. Lebowitz (Eds.). *Stress effects on family caregivers of Alzheimer's patients* (261-277). New York: Springer.

Montgomery, R.J.V., & Borgatta, E.F. (1989). The effects of alternative support strategies on family caregiving. *The Gerontologist, 29,* 457-464.

Montgomery, R.J.V., & Borgatta, E.F. (1989) The effects of alternative support strategies on family caregiving. *The Gerontologist, 29,* 457-464.

Montgomery, R.J.V., & Datwyler, M.M. (1990). Women and men in the caregiving role. *Generations, 14,* 34-38.

Montgomery, R.J.V., & Kosloski, K. (1994). A longitudinal analysis of nursing home placement for dependent elders cared for by spouses vs. adult children. *The Journals of Gerontology, 49,* S62- S74.

Peak, T. (1993). *An examination of the impact of a social support program for spouse caregivers of frail elderly veterans on health care cost.* Unpublished doctoral dissertation. University at Albany, State University of New York, Albany.

Pearlman, D.A., & Crown, W.H. (1992). Alternative sources of social support and their impacts on institutional risk. *The Gerontologist, 32,* 527-535.

Schneider, E.L., & Guralnik, J.M. (1990). The aging of America: Impact on health care costs. *Journal of the American Medical Association, 263,* 2335-2340.

Schopler, J.H., & Galinsky, M.J. (1993). Support groups as open systems: A model for practice and research. *Health and Social Work, 18,* 195-207.

Strawbridge, W.J., & Wallhagan, M.I. (1991). Impact of family conflict on adult child caregivers. *The Gerontologist, 31,* 770-777.

Thompson, E., Futterman, A. Gallagher-Thompson, D., Rose, J., & Lovett, S. (1993). Social support and caregiving burden in family caregivers of frail elders. *Journal of Gerontology, 48,* S245-S254.

Tonti, M. (1988). Relationships among adult siblings who care for their aged parents. In M.D. Kahn, & K.G. Lewis (Eds.), *Siblings in therapy: Lifespan and clinical issues.* (pp.417-434). New York: Columbia University Press.

Toseland, R.W. (in press). *Group Work with Older Adults.* 2nd Edition. New York: Springer.

Toseland, R.W., & Rossiter, C. (1989). Group interventions to support family caregivers: A review and analysis. *The Gerontologist, 29,* 438-448.

Toseland, R.W., Rossiter, C. & Labrecque, M. (1989a). The effectiveness of two kinds of support groups for caregivers. *Social Service Review, 63,* 415-432.

Toseland, R.W., Rossiter, C., & Labrecque, M. (1989b). The effectiveness of peer-led and professionally led groups to support caregivers. *The Gerontologist, 29,*465-471.

Toseland, R., Smith, G.C., & McCallion, P. (in press). Supporting the "family" in family caregiving. In G. Smith, S.S. Tobin, B.A. Robertson-Tchabo, & P. Power (Eds.), *Enabling Aging Families: Directions for practice and policy.* Newbury Park, CA: Sage.

Townsend, A.L., & Noelker, L.S. (1987). The impact of family relationships on perceived caregiving effectiveness. In T. H. Brubaker (Ed.), *Aging, health, and family.* (pp. 80-99). Newbury Park, CA: Sage.

Weiss, R. S. (1974). The provisions of social relationships. In Z. Rubin (Ed.), *Doing unto others* (pp. 17-26). Englewood Cliffs, NJ: Prentice-Hall.

Zarit, S.H., Anthony, C.R., & Boutselis, M. (1987). Interventions with caregivers of dementia patients: Comparison of two approaches. *Psychology and Aging, 2,* 225-232.

Zarit, S. H., & Teri, L. (1991). Interventions and services for family caregivers. In K. W. Schaie (Ed.), *Annual review of gerontology and geriatrics* (Vol. 11, pp. 287-310). New York: Springer.

Evaluating Process, Outcome, and Satisfaction in Community-Based Cancer Support Groups

Myra Glajchen
Randy Magen

SUMMARY. This paper presents an investigation into the process, outcome and satisfaction in three types of cancer support groups: patients with cancer, bereaved spouses and other relatives. The groups followed a model similar to that of Spiegel and Spira's supportive-expressive groupwork (1991). At post-test 392 clients completed a group process and consumer satisfaction questionnaire. In addition, 77 clients also completed the Brief Symptom Inventory (Derogatis & Melisaratos, 1983) as a pre- and post-test. The Brief Symptom Inventory data indicated clients were able to achieve more optimal emotional functioning following support group participation. Patients were the least satisfied of the three conditions and bereaved spouses the most satisfied. Recommendations are offered for screening, group composition, and future research.

INTRODUCTION

A great deal of attention has been directed toward psychosocial intervention for cancer patients, especially through support and

Myra Glajchen, DSW, is Director of Research, Cancer Care, Inc., 1180 Avenue of the Americas, New York, NY 10036. Randy Magen, PhD, is Assistant Professor, Columbia University School of Social Work, 622 West 113 Street, New York, NY 10025.

The authors wish to thank Allen Levine for his enduring support, and Kathleen Dimock for her assistance with this project.

[Haworth co-indexing entry note]: "Evaluating Process, Outcome, and Satisfaction in Community-Based Cancer Support Groups." Glajchen, Myra, and Randy Magen. Co-published simultaneously in *Social Work with Groups* (The Haworth Press, Inc.) Vol. 18, No. 1, 1995, pp. 27-40; and: *Support Groups: Current Perspectives on Theory and Practice* (ed: Maeda J. Galinsky, and Janice H. Schopler) The Haworth Press, Inc., 1995, pp. 27-40. Single or multiple copies of this article are available from The Haworth Document Delivery Center [1-800-342-9678, 9:00 a.m. - 5:00 p.m. (EST)].

27

psychoeducational groups. Experimental outcome studies from academic centers have shown that support groups improve the quality of life for cancer patients (Cella and Yellen, 1993; Spiegel, Bloom and Yalom, 1981), and their ability to cope with the consequences of the disease (Cain, Kohorn, Quinlan, Latimer, & Schwartz, 1986; Spiegel and Bloom, 1983). Similarly, through their participation in psychoeducational groups, where education and support are provided simultaneously, patients demonstrate improved attitudes toward treatment as well as enhanced coping (Feldman, 1993; Fawzy, Fawzy, Hyun, Elashoff, Guthrie, Fahey, & Morton, 1993; Fawzy, Cousins, Fawzy, Kemeny, Elashoff & Morton, 1990; Heinrich & Schag, 1985).

In spite of this impressive body of empirical evidence, several gaps in the literature diminish the clinical utility of these outcome studies. First, despite the proliferation of support groups to help people facing various life crises including cancer, an integrated conceptual framework to guide practice and research has lagged behind (Schopler & Galinsky, 1993). Secondly, the most widely publicized studies have been implemented in tightly controlled methodological environments, where group composition, group goals, and leader techniques could be directly monitored. It is unclear whether the outcomes reported in randomized clinical trials readily transfer to the less structured milieu of a community service agency. The absence of systematic evaluation of group outcomes in community-based support groups has been noted by several researchers (Cella, Sarafian, Snider, Yellen & Winicour, 1993; Schopler & Galinsky, 1993). The few studies published to date have tended to present global, impressionistic and overly positive outcomes. In a more rigorous study, Cella and his associates demonstrated the psychosocial benefits of support group participation for 77 cancer patients following an 8 week community-based support group. The authors of this study urge others to study the effectiveness of such groups, recognizing the importance of quality control and replication (Cella et al., 1993).

Thirdly, the vast majority of support group research in cancer has focused exclusively on cancer patients, de-emphasizing the reality that psychosocial treatment in cancer must include relatives, both during the illness and after the patient's death. This reality is especially critical for social workers, whose mandate it is to bring the person-in-environment perspective to the health care team. Spouses and relatives of cancer patients have been shown to display higher rates of depression, anxiety, illness and medical visits than the general population (Vachon, Freedman, Formo, Rogers, Lyall, & Freeman, 1977). Studies have also shown that the recently bereaved represent a large, at-risk population for future psychosocial dysfunction (Yalom and Vinogradov, 1988). Bereaved spouses and children who have lost a parent to cancer can develop chronic maladaptive coping responses if the process of grieving is incomplete. Yet, evaluation of groups for relatives of cancer patients has been rare (Heinrich and Schag, 1985; Yalom and Vinogradov, 1988).

This article reports the results of a pilot study into the process, outcome and satisfaction of a support group program operated by a large social service agency (Cancer Care, Inc.) located in New York, New Jersey and Connecticut. The conclusions generated are applicable to community social service and mental health agencies. Further, the recommendations have both clinical and research utility.

Group Format. Cancer Care provides three core support groups—for patients, relatives and bereaved spouses of deceased patients. Each group series runs for eight weeks, with closed membership after the second week. The agency is staffed by 35 Masters' level social workers and six social work graduate student interns, each of whom is expected to lead a support group. Individual and peer supervision of group facilitators concentrate on group dynamics, skill-building and discussion of common group themes.

Groups are comprised of six to eight group members, prescreened by the group facilitator. Potential group members are screened twice before entering a group. First, they are assessed by an intake social worker, who refers them to an appropriate group. Secondly, the group facilitator conducts an assessment with the client, either face-to-face or over the telephone. Screening is used to orient group members to the agency and the group structure, to review expectations, and to assess the client's capacity for listening and relating. Clients who are extremely depressed, physically debilitated, or overtly psychotic may be screened out of the group.

Group facilitators are trained in the agency's model of group support, which is similar to Spiegel and Spira's (1991) supportive-expressive approach for women with metastatic breast cancer. In keeping with the supportive-expressive approach, Cancer Care's agency model emphasizes current patient concerns, active exploration by group members, and helping others. However, Cancer Care's model of group support is different in that it is used with all cancer patients as well as relatives. Cancer Care's groups place less emphasis on changing behavior or the willingness to change; agenda items tend to be generated by group members rather than the group leader; and groups are provided for family members as well as cancer patients themselves. In the patient groups, weekly agenda items include the emotional impact of the illness, the meaning of the illness to the patient, relationship difficulties, problems of isolation and intimacy, communication problems with health care providers, and cancer-specific concerns (Spiegel & Spira, 1991). The relatives' support groups are similar, but with more emphasis on caregiver stress, stress management, survivors' guilt, and family communication. Finally, bereavement groups are offered to recently bereaved spouses. The most commonly discussed themes in the bereavement groups are loneliness, loss, role change, and identity as a widow/er.

Cancer Care's groups are defined as a support group, in that they are voluntary, member-centered, based upon mutual aid and led by a professionally trained group facilitator (Schopler and Galinsky, 1993). While agenda topics tend to emanate from group members, the facilitator has specific responsibilities to promote group cohesion, provide structure and information, and encourage reciprocal helping relationship among members (Cella and Yellen, 1993; Schopler and Galinsky, 1993). Socialization of members outside of the group is actively encouraged. Finally, members are given the option of joining another group if unmet needs remain following the eight-week group series.

METHOD

Cancer Care began the process of evaluating its group program in 1988. Through a collaborative relationship with Columbia University, data collection was made more systematic, and data analysis was more refined. In this study, upon completion of the final group session, participants completed a questionnaire which inquired about group processes and consumer satisfaction. The group evaluation questionnaire, specifically designed for this study, consisted of 47 questions divided into five sections. The first section collected data on the client's demographic characteristics. The second section, comprised of 10 questions, inquired about the client's attendance, other sources of social support, and experiences prior to entering the group. Section three of the questionnaire included 12 questions about group processes such as, "Group members provided me with emotional support" and "Group members helped me to realize that other people experience problems similar to mine." The fourth part of the survey explored the client's satisfaction with the group leader. The final portion of the questionnaire contained three consumer satisfaction questions and two open-ended questions asking what the client liked and disliked about the group sessions. All of the questions in sections three and four of the survey were answered using a five-point Likert scale with these anchors for the numerical ratings: 1 "strongly disagree," 2 "slightly disagree," 3 "slightly agree," 4 "moderately agree" and 5 "strongly agree." This instrument takes approximately 15 minutes to complete. From August 1992 through June 1993 all group leaders were asked to administer the Group Evaluation Questionnaire to group members after the last group session. Group Evaluation Questionnaire data were collected from 392 clients who participated in 63 different groups.

Halfway through the study, it was decided to introduce the Brief Symptom Inventory as a pre-post measure of change. This 53-item self-report symptom checklist evaluates nine subscales of distress as well as three global indices of distress. The Brief Symptom Inventory has demonstrated validity and reliability, including use with cancer patients (Derogatis & Melisaratos, 1983). For example, Zabora, Smith-Wilson, Fetting and Enterline (1990) found that the Brief Symptom Inventory could predict future psychosocial distress of cancer patients with 86% accuracy. From February 1993 through June of 1993, 77 clients completed the Brief Symptom Inventory at pre-test and post-test.

Data reported in this study do not include clients who dropped out of treatment. While systematic data on dropouts was not collected, in general it appears that in both relative and patient groups, one client left the group prematurely. Clients tended not to dropout of the bereavement groups. Furthermore, the data collection process, which was carried out by the line social work staff, resulted in what is best termed a convenience sample.

RESULTS

One-half of the 392 clients who completed the post group satisfaction survey were members of groups for bereaved relatives; the remaining fifty percent of the sample were almost evenly split between members of patient groups and members of groups for relatives of patients. On average, clients attended 7.5 group sessions and were absent for almost two sessions ($M = 1.95$). The age range of the group members was 20 to 79 years old. The average age of group members in patient groups was 56 years, in relatives' groups, it was 47 years, and in bereavement groups it was 50. Across all three group conditions there were two to three times more female participants than males. The prototypical client in this sample was a 50 year-old caucasian, college-educated woman. However, there were differences between the three group conditions on the demographic characteristics of group members.

Analysis of variance (ANOVA) revealed statistically significant differences between the group conditions on two of the demographic variables. First, the relatives as a group had, on average, the youngest members while patients had the oldest members, F (2, 354) = 9.46, $p < .001$. Second, given the fact that members of one group condition were recently widowed, there were statistically significant differences between the three conditions on the number of people in the client's household, F (2, 354) = 14.79, $p < .001$. None of the other demographic variables revealed any statistically significant differences between the three group conditions.

Information regarding primary diagnosis was collected only from members of the patient group condition. Of the 94 clients, 23 had been diagnosed with breast cancer, 11 with lung cancer, 8 with colon/rectal cancer, 6 with lymphoma, 5 with myeloma, 4 with ovarian cancer, 4 with Hodgkins disease, 3 with leukemia, and 2 each with bladder, sarcoma, renal, and prostate cancer. The remaining 22 patient support group members had other forms of cancer.

Group Satisfaction. The Group Evaluation Questionnaire data revealed that regardless of the group condition, clients were highly satisfied with their support group experience. On a scale of 1, "not at all satisfied" to 5, "very much satisfied" the average rating for the 392 clients was 4.61. Across the three conditions none of the mean ratings on the 23 consumer satisfaction and group process questions was less than 3.30. The most highly rated group characteristic was that of universalization–realizing that others experience problems similar to oneself. Also highly rated were feeling that the group members had provided comfort, emotional support and advice.

A finer grained analysis revealed statistically significant differences between the three conditions, including the one question related to overall satisfaction (Table 1). The patient support group had the lowest mean score on 11 of the 12 statements related to the efficacy of specific group processes. The one exception was a question about the ability of the group to help the client "feel more comfortable about negotiating the health care system." Conversely, the bereavement support group had the highest mean scores on 10 of these 12 statements about group processes. For 8 of these statements there were statistically significant differences, using analysis of variance, between the three group conditions (see Table 1).

Satisfaction ratings for facilitators were generally favorable. Group leaders were most highly rated for establishing a supportive group atmosphere, encouraging group participation, and providing support to group members. They were less highly rated for helping group members to develop problem-solving skills and deal with difficult situations.

Members of the patient support group reported the lowest level of satisfaction on 6 of the 9 consumer satisfaction questions regarding the group leader. An ANOVA revealed that for two of these items–"the group leader helped me to understand my problems" and "the group leader helped me to deal with difficult situations"–patients were significantly less satisfied with the helpfulness of the group leader than were relatives or bereaved spouses (Table 1).

Psychological Distress. To determine whether group participants perceived the support groups as effective in relieving their psychological distress, matched pair t-tests were conducted on the pre-test and post-test scores of the Brief Symptom Inventory (Table 2). The

TABLE 1. Table of Means for Group Evaluation Questionnaire

Group Characteristics	Patient	Relative	Bereavement	Total
	n = 94	n = 101	n = 197	n = 392
Taught me how to ask for help	3.59	3.71	3.94	3.79*
Provided me emotional support	4.36	4.57	4.66	4.56*
Other people experience same problems	4.69	4.80	4.87	4.81*
Comfort for painful feelings	4.41	4.72	4.80	4.69**
Helped me negotiate health care system	4.07	3.72	3.46	3.69**
More able to handle my problems	3.98	4.23	4.35	4.23**
Overcome my sense of helplessness	3.70	4.01	4.06	3.96*
Helped me get over my anger	3.15	3.60	3.62	3.50**
Leader helped me understand my problems	4.24	4.40	4.52	4.42**
Leader helped me with difficult situations	4.14	4.32	4.42	4.33*
Quality of group sessions	4.18	4.52	4.52	4.44**
Overall satisfaction	4.43	4.69	4.66	4.61**

Note. Not a complete listing. Only statistically significant questions are presented.
*$p < .05$. **$p < .01$.

three global indices of the Brief Symptom Inventory (Positive Symptom Total, General Severity Index, and Positive Symptom Distress Index) all were significantly reduced at post-test. In addition, four of the nine subscales of the Brief Symptom Inventory (Psychoticism, Somatization, Depression, and Obsessive-Compulsive) showed statistically significant differences at post-test. Since the sample size for the Brief Symptom Inventory within each support group condition was relatively small, no within-condition or between-condition statistical tests were conducted.

Analysis of the open-ended questions revealed clients' specific likes and dislikes about their group experience. Members particularly liked the opportunity to ventilate their feelings (33%), the "all-in-the-same-boat phenomenon" (30%) and the supportive atmosphere (29%). On the other hand, they complained about group monopolizers (24%); and they disliked membership composition

TABLE 2. Pre-Test/Post-Test Differences on the Brief Symptom Inventory Total Sample (N = 76)

Brief Symptom Inventory Subscale	Pre-test		Change from Pre to Post[a]
	M	(sd)	
Positive Symptom Total	26.86	(10.78)	2.12*
General Severity Index	54.13	(31.14)	10.04**
Positive Symptom Distress Index	1.89	(.53)	.25**
Psychoticism Subscale	1.89	(.70)	.22*
Hostility Subscale	1.80	(.64)	.20
Anxiety Subscale	1.52	(.66)	− .15
Somatization Subscale	1.72	(.61)	.22**
Phobic Anxiety Subscale	1.67	(.67)	.18
Paranoid Ideation Subscale	1.66	(.68)	.15
Depression Subscale	2.27	(.73)	.41**
Obsessive-Compulsive Subscale	1.96	(.81)	.23**
Interpersonal Sensitivity Subscale	1.71	(.69)	.17

[a]results are for matched pair two tail t-tests

*$p < .05$. ** $p < .01$.

when others were different from themselves in terms of age, diagnosis, or stage of illness (20%). Finally, several members disliked the short term nature of the group which ended regardless of their need for on-going support (26%). For example, when termination corresponded to an important milestone one client wrote, "I disliked the duration of the group sessions. We ended right before Thanksgiving and Christmas, unfortunately adding another loss to my life when I didn't need it." Similarly, another client commented, "I would have liked the group to continue, for both parents and children, until after the holidays."

In sum, the data revealed that members of these support groups were very satisfied with their participation. Furthermore, the outcome data, the Brief Symptom Inventory, indicated that group members were less distressed after having participated in the support groups. Analyses between support group conditions on the group process and consumer satisfaction data showed that members of the patient support groups were the least satisfied while members of the bereavement group condition were the most satisfied.

DISCUSSION

This study provides preliminary data which indicates that clients are able to achieve more optimal emotional functioning as a result of group participation in a community-based support group program. The group process data point to differences among the three conditions in members' perceptions of the efficacy of certain group processes. The patient support groups perceived the lowest levels of provision of emotional support and universality. The bereavement groups, on the other hand, reported the highest levels of these group process attributes. It seems that the crisis involved in bereavement may be more amenable to participation in a time-limited support group than the life-long shadow caused by a diagnosis of cancer.

For the person with cancer, the stressor of the illness tends to be ongoing, with crisis points at diagnosis, at time of treatment cessation, at recurrence, around anniversary dates and during the terminal phase of life. These upheavals necessitate continual physical and psychological adjustment. Researchers have estimated the prevalence of psychosocial distress among cancer patients to be as high as 23% to 50% (Gordon, Freidenbergs, Diller, Hibbard, Wolf, Levine, Lipkins, Ezrachi, & Lucido, 1980). Moreover, it has been found that these heightened levels of distress do not always recede with time. In contrast, bereavement and caring for a relative with cancer are time-limited, normative tasks, for which one might expect improvement over time (Vachon et al. 1977).

It has been argued that the crucial ingredient in successful support groups are "group bonds" (Schopler & Galinsky, 1993). Responses to open-ended questions from clients suggest that attention to those group processes which promote group cohesion may be of primary importance to support group members. For example, one client wrote, "It was the people in the group that was the most important and satisfying. The group leader was OK but wasn't as important as the group. We helped one another because we understood our mutual problems and feelings."

The subtle differences between the group conditions on perceptions of group processes suggest several considerations for both practitioners and researchers. These data indicate that it is important to examine not only group outcomes but also group processes. If we had confined ourselves to questions of global satisfaction and outcome, these different perceptions of group process among the patient, relative and bereavement groups would have been lost.

These differences offer ways in which the patient support group experience could be made more valuable. By forming patient groups where members share a diagnosis and stage of illness it is likely that strong group cohesion would be fostered early on. Given that most groups hate to end, group members need to learn and transfer the skills for obtaining emotional support from the group into their own support networks. Of the 97 responses to the question of what support group members disliked, 20% were related to group membership. For example, one client wrote, "Unfortunately 4 patients died during the time our group met. Since I am at a different stage, the group was inappropriate for me." Finally, one client remarked:

> People with different forms of cancer have different problems and needs. [I] would prefer concentration on specific types of cancer. Also people in different stages of treatment. I am most interested in other women who are coping with what I am also coping with–preferably the same stage.

In fact, other researchers have found that homogenous group membership and close identification with the cancer experience promote high internal group cohesion. Gordon et al. (1980) found in their study of 157 breast, lung and melanoma patients, that each diagnostic site was associated with separate clinical issues. These included concerns related to body image, different types of treatment and different patterns of recovery. It is possible that patients cannot overcome these differences and move toward altruism in a short-term group. Wherever possible, cancer patient groups should be established for single diagnostic groups, with attention to site and stage of disease. It is also probable that stage of illness and diagnosis are salient factors in the composition of relatives' groups.

Perhaps the most striking finding of this study was the reduction in psychological distress after group participation. This is borne out by other researchers who have shown that support groups can promote coping and prevent psychological deterioration. Spiegel and his colleagues (1981) demonstrated lower mood disturbance and fewer maladaptive coping responses in metastatic breast cancer patients who participated in a one-year group treatment program. Although fewer studies exist for families of cancer patients, comparable benefits were found by Wellisch, Mosher and Van Scoy (1978) when they provided family group therapy in a private oncology practice.

Limitations and Recommendations. This study suggests several avenues for future research. First, as has been pointed out by others, information should be collected from those clients who have negative experiences in support groups and who drop-out (Galinsky & Schopler, 1994 in press). The data presented here may be biased in that only those who finished the group completed questionnaires. In addition, although the surveys were anonymous, clients may have felt that they were reporting to their own group facilitator, and this may have curbed their ability to be critical. Also, it was up to group facilitators to collect the Group Evaluation Questionnaires and Brief Symptom Inventories during the last group session. It is not known whether individual group members refused to complete surveys, or whether facilitators failed to turn in overly negative evaluation forms.

Secondly, while this study attempted to overcome a criticism of many other group intervention studies by collecting group process data, the reliability and validity of the instrument used in this investigation have yet to be tested.

Third, given the proliferation of community-based support groups today, it is essential to evaluate their effectiveness. Initially, such attempts may be met with resistance, given the emphasis on service provision in such settings. To reduce bias, it might be preferable to have a research assistant administer the survey rather than place responsibility for data collection on clinicians. However, in the current study, the involvement of agency staff in administering the survey instruments helped to integrate evaluation into the group program. Moreover, the survey instruments themselves were used as a source of clinical information both by line staff and supervisors. The opportunity to receive direct feedback following an eight-week support group served as a reinforcer for group facilitators, while their supervisors utilized the written evaluations to improve the practice of their supervises.

Finally, the successful collaboration between a community agency (Cancer Care) and an academic institution (Columbia) could be replicated elsewhere. The community social service agency provides a rich, natural environment for data collection, while the university setting offers scientific and methodological expertise. In order to motivate the group leaders to administer the survey instruments, the co-operation of the administrative staff and especially the group coordinator were essential. The process of data collection had to be monitored, and group leaders had to be frequently reminded to implement the procedure by their Director of Research. Once data collection for this pilot investigation was complete, the authors presented the findings at a staff development meeting. This generated much enthusiasm and discussion, probably ensuring compliance with future group evaluation efforts.

The rapid proliferation of cancer support groups has been a response to client need and consumer demand. Coupled with these factors has been the movement of cancer treatment from highly specialized hospital settings into the home and community. This pilot study represents the efforts of one community-based agency to move beyond practice wisdom and research insight. The agency-gathered data indicate that support group clients were highly satisfied with their group experience and that group participation reduced emotional distress. Furthermore, the results from this study have pointed the agency in the direction for improving clinical practice and making their support groups more responsive to the members' diverse needs.

REFERENCES

Cain, E., Kohorn, E., Quinlan, D., Latimer, K., & Schwartz, P. (1986). Psychosocial benefits of a cancer support group. *Cancer, 57* (1), 183-189.

Cella, D. F. and Yellen, S. (1993). Cancer support groups: The state of the art. *Cancer Practice, 1* (1), 56-61.

Cella, D. F., Sarafian, B., Snider, P. R., Yellen, S. B., & Winicour, P. (1993). Evaluation of a community-based cancer support group. *Psycho-Oncology, 2,* 123-132.

Derogatis, L. R. & Melisaratos, N. (1983). The Brief Symptom Inventory (BSI): An introductory report. *Psychology of Medicine, 13* (3), 595-605.

Fawzy, F. I., Fawzy, N. W., Hyun, C. S., Elashoff, R., Guthrie, D., Fahey, J. L., & Morton, D. L. (1993). Malignant melanoma. Effects of an early structured psychiatric intervention, coping, and affective state on recurrence and survival 6 years later. *Archives of General Psychiatry, 50* (9), 681-689.

Fawzy, F., Cousins, N., Fawzy, N., Kemeny, M., Elashoff, R., & Morton, D. (1990). A structured psychiatric intervention for cancer patients: changes over time in methods of coping and affective disturbance. *Archives of General Psychiatry, 47* (8), 720-725.

Feldman, J. S. (1993). An alternative approach: Using multi-disciplinary expertise to support patients with prostate cancer and their families. *Journal of Psychosocial Oncology, 11* (2), 83-93.

Galinsky, M. J. & Schopler, J. (1994). Negative experiences in support groups. *Social Work in Health Care, 20* (1), 77-95.

Gordon, W. A., Freidenbergs, I., Diller, L., Hibbard, M., Wolf, C., Levine, L., Lipkins, R., Ezrachi, O., & Lucido, D. (1980). Efficacy of psychosocial intervention with cancer patients. *Journal of Consulting and Clinical Psychology, 48* (6), 743-759.

Heinrich, R. L., & Schag C. C. (1985). Stress and activity management: Group treatment for cancer patients and spouses. *Journal of Consulting and Clinical Psychology, 53* (4), 439-446.

Schopler, J. H., & Galinsky, M. J. (1993). Support groups as open systems: A model for practice and research. *Health and Social Work, 18* (3), 195-207.

Spiegel, D. & Spira, J. (1991). *Supportive-expressive group therapy: a treatment manual of psychosocial intervention for women with recurrent breast cancer.* Stanford, CA: Stanford University School of Medicine, Psychosocial Treatment Laboratory.

Spiegel, D. & Bloom, J. (1983). Group therapy and hypnosis reduce metastatic breast carcinoma pain. *Psychosomatic Medicine, 45* (4), 333-339.

Spiegel, D., Bloom, J., & Yalom, I. (1981). Group support for patients with metastatic cancer: A randomized outcome study. *Archives of General Psychiatry, 38* (5), 527-533.

Turns, D. M. (1988). Psychosocial factors. In W. L. Donegan, & J. S. Spratt (eds.) *Cancer of the Breast* (3rd ed., pp. 728-738). Philadelphia: W. B. Saunders.

Vachon, M. L. S., Freedman, K., Formo, A., Rogers, J., Lyall, W. A. L., & Freeman, S. J. J. (1977). The final illness in cancer: The widow's perspective. *Canadian Medical Journal, 19*, 1151-1154.

Wellisch, D. K., Mosher, M. B., & Van Scoy, C. (1978). Management of family emotion stress: Family group therapy in a private oncology practice. *International Journal of Group Psychotherapy, 28* (3), 225-231.

Yalom, I. and Vinogradov, S. (1988). Bereavement groups: Techniques and themes. *International Journal of Group Psychotherapy, 38* (4), 419-445.

Zabora, J. R., Smith-Wilson, R., Fetting, J. H., & Enterline, J. P. (1990). An efficient method for psychosocial screening of cancer patients. *Psychosomatics, 31* (2), 192-196.

Women with Postpartum Psychiatric Illness:
A Professionally Facilitated
Support Group

Muki W. Fairchild

SUMMARY. Since the 1990s, many support groups for distressed new mothers have been established. Few of these groups have been described in the literature; most reports are of self-help groups. This paper describes the structure and benefits of an open ended, no fee, professionally facilitated support group established by the Duke Postpartum Support Program. The advantages of having a facilitator with mental health training in serving women with moderate to severe postpartum psychiatric illness are emphasized. Group problems are identified and the results of a satisfaction survey supportive of clinical impressions are included. *[Single or multiple copies of this article are available from The Haworth Document Delivery Service: 1-800-342-9678, 9:00 a.m. - 5:00 p.m. (EST).]*

Following the birth of a baby, approximately 1 out of every 10 new mothers will experience a major psychiatric illness (O'Hara &

Muki W. Fairchild, CCSW, is Head, Division of Psychiatric Social Work, Department of Psychiatry, Duke University Medical Center, Box 3037, Durham, NC 27710.

The author wishes to thank Bill Meyer, MSW, founder and co-director of the Duke Postpartum Support Program for his support; Charles McNamara, social work intern, for his work on the satisfaction survey; and Linda Watkins for manuscript preparation.

[Haworth co-indexing entry note]: "Women with Postpartum Psychiatric Illness: A Professionally Facilitated Support Group." Fairchild, Muki W. Co-published simultaneously in *Social Work with Groups* (The Haworth Press, Inc.) Vol. 18, No. 1, 1995, pp. 41-53; and: *Support Groups: Current Perspectives on Theory and Practice* (ed: Maeda J. Galinsky, and Janice H. Schopler) The Haworth Press, Inc., 1995, pp. 41-53. Single or multiple copies of this article are available from The Haworth Document Delivery Center [1-800-342-9678, 9:00 a.m. - 5:00 p.m. (EST)].

Zekowski, 1988; Hamilton & Harberger, 1993). An event that most women eagerly anticipate can turn into a nightmare for some as depression, anxiety, and even psychosis take over. Women are particularly vulnerable in the postpartum period. Following childbirth, women are more likely to suffer from a major psychiatric disorder, more likely to be referred to a psychiatrist, and more likely to be admitted to a psychiatric hospital than at any other time in their lives (Paffenberger, 1964).

Interventions typically consist of some combination of pharmacotherapy and support or psychotherapy. With the establishment of Depression after Delivery (DAD), a national self-help organization founded in 1985, and Postpartum Support International, founded in 1987, large numbers of telephone hot lines and support groups have been formed for distressed new mothers in the United States (Berchtold & Burrough, 1990). These groups tend to have the characteristics of self help groups (N. Berchtold, personal communication, April, 1994) and only a few have been described in the literature (Abriola, 1990; Fleming, Klein & Corter, 1992). The literature on group psychotherapy or professionally facilitated support groups with this population is equally sparse, with just a handful of reports (Gruen, 1993; Morris, 1987).

After an overview of postpartum psychiatric disorders, a description of an open ended, no fee, professionally facilitated support group established by the Duke Postpartum Support Program in 1991 is provided. Important group themes, benefits for members, and group problems are addressed. Overall, the results of a satisfaction survey validate clinical impressions that women with moderate to severe postpartum psychiatric illness can benefit from this type of support group experience.

POSTPARTUM PSYCHIATRIC DISORDERS

Under the best of circumstances, caring for a new baby can be stressful. The stress scale in the *Diagnostic and Statistical Manual of Mental Disorders* (DSM-III-R) rates the birth of a first child as "severe stress," equal to that of a marital divorce. Learning to function on less sleep, finding reliable child care, coping with a changed body image, and for the working mother, reconciling the conflicting roles of mother, wife, and employee (Downey, 1991) are challenging tasks. For the mothers who experience postpartum mood and anxiety disorders, the tasks become impossible.

Postpartum difficulties are typically divided into three broad categories: the baby or maternity blues, postpartum depression, and postpartum psychosis (Hamilton & Harberger, 1992; O'Hara & Zekowski, 1988; Kendall, Chalmers & Platz, 1987). The symptoms of baby blues, i.e., sadness, irritability, crying, and anxiety, are common, affecting up to 85% of all new mothers. Fortunately, they are short lived, typically subsiding by the end of the second week after birth. Women with baby blues benefit from time and support from family and friends; the majority require no professional treatment. Yet some of these women do go on to develop a full-blown major depression or anxiety disorder, and they are joined by others who appeared well immediately after delivery but who subsequently become depressed and anxious as the weeks go by.

Major depression and anxiety disorders affect anywhere from 10-15% of all new mothers. These women may suffer with some or all of the well-known symptomatology so typical of a major depression: diminished energy, multiple physical symptoms, difficulty concentrating, suicidal ideation, loss of interest, fatigue, sleep and appetite disturbances, and agitation or psychomotor retardation. Certain risk factors have been implicated with this group of disorders, among them marital tension, low levels of social support, and previous episodes of depression (Boyce, Hickie & Parker, 1991; O'Hara, 1986; O'Hara, 1991). A significant subgroup also has severe, intrusive and ego-dystonic ruminations about harm coming to the baby, a syndrome that is now being called postpartum obsessive compulsive disorder (Sichel, Cohen, Dimmock & Rosenbaum, 1993). Professional treatment for these conditions is indicated, and usually involves some combination of pharmacotherapy, support, and/or psychotherapy in an outpatient, day hospital or inpatient setting.

Postpartum psychosis, the most severe of the postpartum disorders, is rare, with a prevalence rate of 1-2 births per 1000. It typically occurs within two weeks after childbirth. Common symptoms are delusions and hallucinations, often with a religious theme. Postpartum psychosis is considered a medical emergency, requiring immediate medical intervention and often hospitalization. Women with a previous postpartum or other psychosis, or a family history of bi-polar disorder seem to be especially vulnerable.

Postpartum psychiatric illness can have devastating consequences for all members of the family. Depressed mothers have more trouble parenting and their children may show delays in cognitive and social development as well as a higher rate of behavioral disturbances (Downey & Coyne, 1990; Tronick & Gianino, 1986). Marriages may be adversely affected (Holden, 1991). Even when successfully treated, the woman who has experienced a postpartum disorder is likely to find that her self-esteem remains impaired. Although all mental illness is stigmatizing, an illness that strikes at the heart of the mother-child relationship can damage even an experienced mother's faith in her ability to be a good parent.

THE DEVELOPMENT OF THE DUKE POSTPARTUM SUPPORT GROUP

The idea for a postpartum support program with a no fee support group arose in 1990, as the result of an infant mental health study project at Duke University Medical Center which revealed the need for improved mental health services for new mothers. An affiliation with Depression After Delivery was obtained, and 500 brochures were mailed out to ministers, pediatricians, and obstetricians. Posters were placed throughout the hospital inviting distressed new mothers and their babies to attend a support group.

The actual group began in 1991, with two social work facilitators, (a female MSW senior staff member, and a male graduate intern), and two women, referred by the North Carolina DAD coordinator with severe, advanced depression and obsessive-compulsive symptoms. It took six more months to recruit additional members. The telephone did not begin to ring until the publication of a newspaper article containing an interview with the two group members. Women began to call, saying that they had believed they were alone, too ashamed to seek help. Some were being treated, but had been reluctant to confide in their therapists or husbands, fearing the consequences of such exposure. The calls have not stopped; to date, more than 100 women have called the postpartum support program and 46 have attended the support group.

KEY FEATURES OF THE POSTPARTUM SUPPORT GROUP MODEL

Current conceptualizations of supportive group interventions span a continuum from self-help to support to treatment (Berchtold, 1990; Lieberman and Rosenberg, 1984; Schopler and Galinsky, 1993). The Duke postpartum support group combines features of both support and treatment. These features are described below.

Sponsorship and Access. Since the group is sponsored by a medical center, meetings are held in the outpatient psychiatric clinic of the hospital on the second and fourth Tuesdays of each month, from 6:30 p.m. until 8 p.m. (A day time group was discontinued because of poor attendance). Participation is kept open, so that each woman is welcome to attend as many or as few meetings as she wishes, but access is controlled. Women must undergo a telephone or face-to-face screening. Based on the success of the group experience with the first two members who were initially so ill, membership has been limited to women suffering from the more severe forms of these disorders. They are referred by other health care professionals at Duke, in the community and throughout the state, through DAD, and by word of mouth.

Members. Group size ranges from 2 to 8 women with an average of 5 at each meeting; at least one baby is usually present. Because there are so few support groups for this population in North Carolina, some of the 46 women who have attended the group have travelled considerable distances, ranging from 1 to 4 hours each way. The majority of members have been white, middle class married women, ranging in age from 20 to 41. Five African-American women have participated. Of the 46, 28 have been first time mothers, 10 have had 2 children, 7 have had 3, and 1 woman has had 5. Some of the women have come soon after delivery; many others report delays of months and even years before finding the group. Twelve out of the 46 have been hospitalized at least once for postpartum depression, anxiety, or psychosis; two have been treated in a day hospital program. Since the group takes place in the same building as the inpatient psychiatric service, women who are hospitalized for postpartum psychiatric disorders can, with the consent of their attending physician, be invited and included.

Leader and Control. One professional MSW social work facilitator is always present; the graduate social work intern was not replaced, but the same staff member (the author) has continued to serve as the primary facilitator. When meetings are opened up to families, once or twice a year, the co-director of the program, a male MSW social worker, joins the facilitator. Observers may also attend. Because Duke is a training facility, requests to observe by trainees are common, and the group members have allowed observers, one at a time.

Although control is shared between members and the facilitator, particularly around decisions that affect the group, like permitting observers, the facilitator takes responsibility for beginning, maintaining, and ending the group. These responsibilities include such tasks as: the screening and assessment of prospective group members, arriving early in order to arrange the furniture in the room, starting and ending the group on time, introducing new members, making sure that each member has a turn to talk, managing dominating members, giving out informational packets, and maintaining a current list of resources for the group.

Since the group serves both hospitalized and nonhospitalized women, all with the more severe forms of these disorders, the facilitator must be prepared to assess and manage whatever level of distress arises during the course of a meeting. If a new member is overwhelmed by anxiety or depression, the facilitator must be able to determine whether it is safe for her to return to her home that evening. Similarly, it is the facilitator's role to manage the interactions with an acutely ill, hospitalized woman. The facilitator's professional experience with the assessment and treatment of psychiatric illness is critical in handling these responsibilities.

Group Function and Rules. The group provides a supportive, accepting environment that allows the women to share their experiences and help each other manage better. A typical group begins slowly, as group members often arrive late due to distance and work schedules. The meetings are unstructured with no preset agenda. Chairs are arranged in a circle, making it easier for each woman to take a turn and talk about her situation. When a new member attends, introductions are performed in order to make her feel welcome and included. Each member not only introduces herself by name, but gives the newcomer a brief summary of her illness and her involvement with the group. The new member is also given an opportunity to ask questions of the group in order to gain from the available collective wisdom.

New members may initially be too ill or too distressed to talk. Although confidentiality is requested, no one is pressured to speak, and women are given explicit permission to remain silent if they so choose. Similarly, they are free to speak about their illness in whatever detail they wish. Frightening material is not discouraged.

BENEFITS FOR MEMBERS

Reduction of Isolation. In the words of one woman, "Meeting people like me made me realize I was not alone." Listening to the stories of other women, "You get to know you are not the only one and that you are not crazy." Unlike self-help groups that mix different levels of severity, as a professionally facilitated support group with a more homogenous population we can encourage the telling of a woman's entire story, even the more frightening aspects of her experience.

Unlike treatment groups, however, we encourage extra group contacts and friendships. This is accomplished through the affiliation with DAD and by establishing a telephone network so that a woman in distress can always contact current and past group members by telephone. Members joke about the size of their telephone bills; progress is often measured by a reduction in monthly bills. There are occasional social events. A pot luck supper for members and their families was held to celebrate the group's third anniversary.

Getting Information. The group provides information about many aspects of the illness, including symptoms, risk factors, other possible contributing factors, etiologies, and recurrence rates, as well as ways to cope. Some group members have a tendency to generalize from their experience, attributing their situation to others. Other members are adamantly convinced of a particular etiology, e.g., that their illness is hormonal and has nothing to do with their life situation. In both instances, the facilitator's mental health background allows her to review the relevant literature, emphasizing the multi-factorial nature of the illness as well as the singular uniqueness of each woman and her situation. It is not unusual for a woman to begin to question her family of origin, and discover that her mother or her sister or another female relative had postpartum depression, information of which she had not previously been aware.

Education is critical for women who are experiencing intrusive thoughts. Repeatedly, we have found that a woman has not revealed the presence of these thoughts, fearing them as proof that she is crazy and a bad mother, evidence that could result in child welfare removing her child or abandonment by her husband. It is only when another woman specifically brings up this subject and offers examples about herself, such as imagining knives coming toward her baby's face, that a new member is able to admit that she, too, has had bizarre thoughts.

The women in the group are also eager for information on issues related to the illness, such as child development consequences. Distressed new mothers are understandably concerned about the impact of the illness on their children, so the facilitator must be able to distinguish normal developmental issues from reactions to the maternal illness. Separation issues are common; mothers with intrusive thoughts often cope by hovering over their infants, hoping that bad things will not occur if they are there to ward them off. Others avoid the baby, believing their absence is protective.

Permission for Self Care. The group encourages new mothers to focus and take care of themselves. We focus on the basics–eating and sleeping. Women are encouraged to tell carefully selected family members and friends of their illness and to ask for help, actively and assertively. If they are acutely ill, they are encouraged to put the marriage and the past on hold. As one therapist in the program explains, "When the house is on fire, put the fire out first, then do the rewiring." Medical analogies may be useful in helping a woman accept that she has limits, and in setting realistic expectations for herself and for others. We compare postpartum psychiatric illness to a heart attack, and suggest a woman give herself whatever time is needed in order to get better before she resumes all of her responsibilities.

Support for Treatment. When a woman has not yet sought medical evaluation and treatment, the group can reduce the stigma of seeking help. Many women fear psychotropic medications. Medication is a particularly sensitive issue for lactating mothers. Some mothers have chosen to stop breastfeeding once medication is prescribed; others have continued to nurse successfully. Support for either decision is available, and the facilitator can put a mother struggling with such a dilemma in contact with another woman who has experienced and resolved this conflict, or make an appropriate referral.

Hope for the Future. The group provides hope that women can and do get better. By incorporating members at different stages of the illness, acutely ill mothers are provided role models, proof that they too will recover. This was described by one member: "There were others going through different stages and this was good to see." Another said, "It helped me see where I was, not the best case, not the worst." The recovering mothers can offer a realistic view of the illness, and the time frame for recovery.

The group is there to rejoice with a woman when she begins to recover and feel better, and to note the positive changes, often before she herself has become aware of them. This role was noticed by a member who said, "The group was (my) main link to recovery; I used it as a barometer to judge (my) recovery."

The recovered members are also able to impart some meaning to the experience; a sense that they have actually gained something from the illness–a reordering of priorities and goals–the kind of knowledge achieved only by surviving and mastering pain and trauma. As one recovered woman stated, when describing a later crisis with an adolescent daughter, "Being sick has made me stronger and better able to cope with other things. When I get upset about something, I measure it against what I have gone through and it is never as bad as being sick was."

Supportive Treatment Intervention. Although a support group is *not* a substitute for medical evaluation and treatment, with professional facilitation the group can provide a safe place for a suffering woman to share her worst fears. She learns that intrusive thoughts are a part of the illness, and that thinking about injury to her baby is not the same as having it happen or doing it. This intervention alone can help her feel less guilty and reduce the impact of the illness on her self esteem. The group also provides a safe place to deal with the full range of feelings that are part of the trauma of illness: shame, anger, fear, guilt, and grief. One woman commented, "You didn't have to hide things about your feelings. They understood and you didn't have to feel guilty."

SATISFACTION SURVEY

A telephone survey was conducted in 1993 to assess the level of satisfaction with the group and to see if the facilitators' belief in its efficacy was a view shared by the members. A graduate social work intern not associated with the program contacted 27 women who had attended the group during a specific 18 month period. Letters describing the survey, assuring anonymity, and offering a written rather than a telephone version had been sent out earlier.

The survey consisted of a basic set of twelve questions with four possible additional questions. In addition to gathering some data on attendance, two of the twelve questions were open ended and asked what a woman liked best and least about the group. The remaining ten questions used a five point scale and focused on the woman's satisfaction with the group: the extent to which she felt she had gotten support, information, and help, her level of comfort in the group, and whether she would recommend the group to a friend with similar difficulties. The women were also given the opportunity to make suggestions for improvement.

All 27 women were successfully contacted and 26 (96%) completed the survey. Of those 26, 25 (96%) felt they were able to share their concerns some or almost all of the time, 22 (85%) felt they got either a fair amount or a lot of support for their situation, 19 (73%) felt they had gotten either a fair amount or a lot of information about postpartum problems, and 20 (77%) women felt they had been helped by the group. All but 2 of the 26 women (93%) felt they would either probably or definitely recommend the group to a friend with similar difficulties.

The comments were of particular interest. Cited most frequently as positive features were: meeting others with similar problems (58%), the professional staff associated with the program (50%), and the honesty and openness of the meetings (23%). Cited most frequently as negative features were: the difference in the needs of recovered members and newer members (19%), and not having enough time at meetings (19%). The main suggestions for improvement were to: get the word out and advertise the program (31%), and provide more information and education to group members (19%). Both of these suggestions have been followed. Of critical importance was the validation of the facilitators' belief in the usefulness of the group for this population, thus providing them the necessary feedback and encouragement to continue.

PROBLEMS WITH THE GROUP

Aside from the problems common to most groups, such as dominating members and group size, the main problem in the DAD self-help groups stems from mixing the different populations of distressed mothers, those suffering from baby blues all the way to those recovering from a postpartum psychosis (N. Berchtold, personal communication, April, 1994). In order to serve all of the women, DAD encourages lay facilitators to limit some of the discussion around severe illness and specific treatment regimens. By using a trained facilitator and screening prospective members, we have tried a different approach, limiting our membership and not the discussions.

However, the satisfaction survey did point out another problem with the discussions: meeting the needs of both the acutely ill and the recovered women. As one woman said, "I felt that people who had been coming for a long time and were well into recovery were drained at meetings by people who were new and at the height of their crisis." Another noted that, "It seems very repetitive when new people come in and everyone goes back around with their stuff." The older members were also afraid to speak openly about their concerns, fearing that it might upset newer members.

The facilitator has been able to introduce some modifications in order to address this problem, such as limiting the content of the introductions. Since one of her responsibilities is to monitor the affective tone of the group, she has also been able to assure older members that they could safely focus on their concerns. Nonetheless, the problem of differing needs related to different stages of recovery remains. Although some recovered members do elect to keep coming, if only to reach out to the newer ones, it seems that many simply stop attending on a regular basis when the group no longer meets their needs.

CONCLUSIONS

With the current concern about health care costs, an organization may question the use of a clinician whose time is not directly reimbursed. We believe such a view would be shortsighted, since this model may be useful in either an indemnity fee for service, or a managed care environment. In a fee for service arrangement, it serves to attract a population that is often under- or misdiagnosed, and is willing to travel considerable distances in order to obtain appropriate treatment, thus providing patients for the full continuum of services: inpatient, day hospital, and outpatient. In managed care, as a support and a treatment modality in its own right, this model serves to help manage an often disabling illness in a cost effective way, linking these women with a service that can be accessed either in or out of the hospital.

REFERENCES

Abriola, D. V. (1990). Mothers' perceptions of a postpartum support group. *Maternal Child Nursing Journal, 19*(2), 113-134.

American Psychiatric Association. (1987). *Diagnostic and Statistical Manual of Mental Disorders* (3rd ed., rev.). Washington, DC: Author.

Berchtold, N., & Burrough, M. (1990). Reaching out: Depression after delivery support group network. In *Critical Issues in Perinatal and Women's Health Nursing, Vol. 1* (pp. 385-393). Washington, DC: NAACOG.

Boyce, P., Hickie, I., & Parker, G. (1991). Parents, partners or personality? Risk factors for post-natal depression. *Journal of Affective Disorders, 21*, 245-255.

Downey, G., & Coyne, J. (1990). Children of depressed parents: Integrative review. *Psychological Bulletin, 108*(1), 1-27.

Fleming, A. S., Klein, E., & Corter, C. (1992). The effects of a social support group on depression, maternal attitudes and behavior in new mothers. *Journal of Child Psychology, 33*(4), 685-698.

Gruen, D. S. (1993). A group psychotherapy approach to postpartum depression. *International Journal of Group Psychotherapy, 43*(2), 191-203.

Hamilton, J. A., & Harberger, P. N. (Eds.) (1992). *Postpartum Psychiatric Illness.* Philadelphia: University of Pennsylvania Press.

Holden, J. M. (1991). Postnatal depression: Its nature, effects, and identification using the edinburgh postnatal depression scale. *Birth, 18*(4), 211-221.

Kendall, R. E., Chalmers, J. C., & Platz, C. (1987). Epidemiology of puerperal psychoses. *British Journal of Psychiatry, 150*, 662-673.

Lieberman, M. A. (1990). A group therapist perspective on self-help groups. *International Journal of Psychotherapy, 40*(3), 251-278.

Morris, J. B. (1987). Group psychotherapy for prolonged postnatal depression. *British Journal of Medical Psychology, 60*, 279-281.

O'Hara, M. W. (1986). Social support, life events, and depression during pregnancy and the puerperium. *Archives of General Psychiatry, 43*, 569-573.

O'Hara, M. W., Schlechte, J. A., Lewis, D. A., & Varner, M. W. (1991). Controlled prospective study of postpartum mood disorders: Psychological, environmental, and hormonal variables. *Journal of Abnormal Psychology, 100*(2), 151-155.

O'Hara, M. W., Zekowski, E. M. (1988). Postpartum depression: A comprehensive review. In R. Kumar & I. F. Brockington (Eds.), *Motherhood and Mental Illness, Vol 2* (pp. 17-63). London: Wright.

Paffenberger, R. S. (1964). Epidemiological aspects of postpartum mental illness. *British Journal of Preventive and Social Medicine, 18*, 189-195.

Rosenberg, P. P. (1984). Support groups: A special therapeutic entity. *Small Group Behavior, 15*(2), 173-186.

Schopler, J. H., & Galinsky, M. J. (1993). Support groups as open systems: A model for practice and research. *Health and Social Work, 18*(3), 195-207.

Sichel, D., Cohen, L. S., Dimmock, J. A., & Rosenbaum, J. F. (1993). Postpartum obsessive compulsive disorder: A case series. *Journal of Clinical Psychiatry, 54*(4), 156-159.

Tronick, E. Z., & Gianino, A. F. (1986). The transmission of maternal disturbance to the infant. In E. Z. Tronick & T. Field (Eds.), *Maternal Depression and Infant Disturbance* (pp. 61-82). New Directions for Child Development, No. 34.

The Unique Social Ecology of Groups: Findings from Groups for African Americans Affected by Sickle Cell Disease

Kathryn D. Kramer

Kermit B. Nash

SUMMARY. Ecological theory has been embraced by many professionals in social work, psychology, and other human service disciplines. Researchers have found the social ecological paradigm useful in understanding the process of group development. Using data from a research project on 123 groups across the United States organized for persons affected by sickle cell disease, this paper will show how ecological theory can be used to study group differences and similarities. This study will form the basis for demonstrating that each group is unique within a community, as diversity among individual members and the social ecology of groups vary. A discussion will follow showing how practitioners or resource persons for groups must respond to the diversity between and within groups. *[Single or multiple copies of this article are available from The Haworth Document Delivery Service: 1-800-342-9678, 9:00 a.m. - 5:00 p.m. (EST).]*

Kathryn D. Kramer, PhD, is Clinical Assistant Professor and Kermit B. Nash, PhD, is Professor, School of Social Work, The University of North Carolina, CB # 3560, Chapel Hill, NC 27599.

This study was funded by the Heart, Lung, and Blood Institute of the National Institutes of Health (Grant #5P60 HL283292-10).

[Haworth co-indexing entry note]: "The Unique Social Ecology of Groups: Findings from Groups for African Americans Affected by Sickle Cell Disease." Kramer, Kathryn D., and Kermit B. Nash. Co-published simultaneously in *Social Work with Groups* (The Haworth Press, Inc.) Vol. 18, No. 1, 1995, pp. 55-65; and: *Support Groups: Current Perspectives on Theory and Practice* (ed: Maeda J. Galinsky, and Janice H. Schopler) The Haworth Press, Inc., 1995, pp. 55-65. Single or multiple copies of this article are available from The Haworth Document Delivery Center [1-800-342-9678, 9:00 a.m. - 5:00 p.m. (EST)].

55

A nationwide study of groups for persons affected by sickle cell disease was conducted. Approximately 99% of the group members were African American. Using ecological theory as a foundation, this study was designed to explore the interrelationship of group and individual characteristics. Findings showed as many differences among groups as similarities, reflecting the constellation of individual and environmental variations among communities. These findings support the notion that groups form a unique social niche within a community (Maton, 1989; 1994).

One of the first issues to resolve in this study involved the issue of defining groups. Defining or typing groups according to group function was considered (Levy 1976; 1979). It quickly became evident that this strategy was not feasible. Groups had multiple functions and activities, as the data presented in this paper will demonstrate. Distinct activities could not be attributed to any one group. Although similar activities could be noted across groups, the frequency and duration of these activities (e.g., sharing personal experiences, conducting social activities, advocating for changes in the community) varied considerably.

The difficulty of defining and typing groups has been thoroughly discussed in the literature (Levy, 1976). Schopler and Galinsky (1993) have provided a clear review of the defining characteristics that help one label a group as either self-help, support, or treatment. Although there is less confusion over what constitutes treatment groups, there is some debate over the distinctions between self-help groups and support groups. Within the self-help literature, the terms mutual assistance and mutual help have been adopted and are used more frequently to reflect the mutual sharing and help that is given and received by group members (Levine, 1987; Maton, 1993). This paper will adopt the term mutual assistance to refer to all sickle cell groups, as that term reflects the blurring of lines between self-help and support groups and more aptly mirrors the kinds of groups participating in this study.

The observed differences noted in this study at the individual, group, and community levels certainly were compatible with ecological theory. As a search for a meta-theory on group development continues, it does seem that the ecological paradigm or a systems perspective is pervasive. Scholars discuss how multiple factors interrelate and groups develop accordingly (Kramer & Nash, 1992; Maton, 1994). Factors such as (1) member characteristics (e.g., age, gender, race); (2) focal problem of group; (3) member needs and reasons for attending group; (4) members' and leaders' styles of interactions; (5) the communities in which the groups reside; (6) the services and resources available to the groups; and (7) the cultural, political, and economic factors predominant in the environment are all discussed. The ecological paradigm is certainly compatible with the work of Schopler and Galinsky (1993) as they proposed an open systems model for guiding interventions and evaluations with support groups that included an examination of environmental conditions, participant group characteristics, group conditions, and outcomes.

Regardless of the definition used to type a group or the theoretical perspective of the researcher, a review of outcome studies in the literature shows that the main focus of research on support groups, mutual assistance groups, or treatment groups has been at the individual level. For example, many studies have focused on member-well being and benefits of participation in groups (Bednar & Kaul, 1978; Kurtz, 1994; Lipson, 1982; Schubert & Borkman, 1994; Videka-Sherman, 1982). Others have attempted to move beyond the individual level of analysis and have explored helping mechanisms in groups (Borman, 1976; Levy, 1976; 1979; Nash & Kramer, 1993; 1994) and the social climate of groups (Levine, 1987; Luke, Roberts, & Rappaport, 1993; Maton, 1989). Research models that attempt to examine the interrelationships among the different levels (i.e., individual, group, and social) are quite complex and limited applications of a multi-level model are noted (Maton, 1993; 1994). Although useful for increasing our understanding group development, the complexity of the ecological paradigm can be paralyzing for practitioners and researchers. It is hoped that this study will show a useful application of the theory and an attempt by researchers to move beyond the individual level of analysis.

METHODS

A qualitative, longitudinal study of sickle cell mutual assistance groups was conducted from 1988-1993. A nationwide survey was conducted using telephone and mail survey techniques to locate all groups organized to help individuals affected by sickle cell disease. Once located, group leaders responded to a structured mail survey. Of 134 groups located across the United States, leaders of 123 groups (91.8%) participated in the project and provided information on group structure and function. Also, individuals ($n = 61$) from 15 groups across 10 states responded to a structured mail survey and provided demographic data and endorsed a list of reasons for their participation in sickle cell mutual assistance groups. Descriptive findings using cross-sectional data sampling methods will be reported in this paper. Following an ecological model, variable selection provided individual and group level data and included: (1) information regarding group structure (including leadership patterns and professional involvement, member characteristics, and structure of meetings); (2) a description of group activities; (3) a summary of special features of groups, and (4) a list of reasons individual members attended group meetings. For the variables noting group activities and special features of groups, a structured list was provided and responses were offered on a 4 point Likert scale (never, almost never, sometimes, and very often). To offer a description of the functions of these groups, the categories "sometimes" and "very often" were collapsed and percentages were reported in this paper. However, the responses on the Likert scale showed wide variation in frequency of activities and special features of groups. This data forms the basis for the discussion on the uniqueness of groups.

FINDINGS ON SICKLE CELL MUTUAL ASSISTANCE GROUPS

Structure of Groups

Professionals were involved in the formation of 86.7% ($n = 104$) of the groups. However, it appeared that the role of the professional or facilitator changed as the groups evolved. The motivation for or conditions surrounding these changes were not measured. At the time of the interview, 27.3% of the groups ($n = 33$) were still led by a professional; 38.8% ($n = 47$) were co-led (leadership was shared between a member and a professional; and 29.8% ($n = 36$) of all groups were member led with no professional involvement. Overall, 66.1% ($n = 80$) of all groups still had some level of professional involvement in the leadership of the groups.

Groups met and were structured in such a way that at any given meeting, group activities could shift according to member attendance and needs. Most groups met on a monthly basis (54.9%; $n = 67$), while 12.3% met twice a month ($n = 15$). A typical meeting would have an average of 11 members in attendance ($SD = 6.8$). In general, there were more females than males attending groups, with a ratio of close to 2:1. The age of members ranged from 19-68 years ($M = 37$; $SD = 11$). All groups maintained an open-ended membership policy, so at any given meeting, membership characteristics could vary (e.g., new members entered groups constantly, and thus, the needs and the dynamics of the groups shifted from meeting to meeting).

An examination of membership showed that groups could be categorized into four groupings according to who attended meetings. These categories included: (1) 52.8% of the groups ($n = 65$) were organized for a mixed group (i.e., adults and children with sickle cell disease and their significant others); (2) 18.7% of the groups ($n = 23$) were for parents of children with sickle cell disease; (3) 16.3% of the groups ($n = 20$) were for adults with sickle cell disease; and (4) 12.2% of the groups ($n = 15$) were for adolescents with sickle cell disease.

Special Features and Supportive Roles of Groups

Group leaders identified what they thought were special or "unique" features of the individual groups and also reported on the supportive roles and activities of these groups. As previously noted, responses were given on a Likert scale, and this data showed considerable variation in frequency of special features and activities among groups. However, when the categories "sometimes" and "very often" were combined, group functions could be described. Among the special features, more than half of all of the groups reported engaging in the following: (1) advocating for change (57.9%; $n = 70$); (2) providing speakers for other groups (57.0%;

$n = 69$); (3) having a phone help system (55.8%; $n = 67$); (4) providing transportation for other members to group meetings (52.9%; $n = 64$); and, (5) having a buddy system (50.4%; $n = 61$). Group leaders also reported the supportive roles and activities of group members. More than 80% of all the groups in the study reported that group members: (1) gave advice to one another (95.9%; $n = 116$); (2) talked about things that cause stress on the family (95.1%; $n = 116$); (3) talked about very personal feelings (91.0%; $n = 110$); (4) listened to experts talk about sickle cell disease (88.3%; $n = 96$); (5) learned how to deal with emotional issues (87.7%; $n = 107$); and (6) talked about how to recruit members (81.1%; $n = 99$).

Reasons for Participating in Groups

There were many reasons listed by members for participating in group meetings. More than 75% of all participants indicated that they attended the group to: (1) help improve the health care of people with sickle cell disease (90.2%; $n = 55$); (2) learn more about sickle cell disease (86.9%; $n = 53$); (3) to give support to other group members (86.9%; $n = 53$); and (4) to get support from other group members (77.0%; $n = 47$).

DISCUSSION

The Unique Ecology of Groups in Communities

The overlap seen in group activities (e.g., social, emotional, educational, and supportive) and reasons for attending groups supports the notion that mutual assistance groups are involved in similar functions and people choose to join a group for similar reasons. However, an attempt to categorize groups accordingly fails, as there is considerably variability between and within groups regarding the frequency and assumed duration of these events. This observation is critical to our understanding of group diversity as these functions can occur simultaneously, yet to varying degrees in each group. As groups organize around a particular focal problem, group activities respond to the needs of individual members. In turn, the group functions within a given community where cultural, political, economic, and health factors vary. Thus, groups form in response to a need and develop in response to various dynamic processes. As this process continues, the group develops and fills a need within a community. These groups form "alternative social environments" where members feel less isolated and can develop social competencies (Levine, 1987; Maton, 1989).

As each group develops and fills a niche within a community, the social ecology of the group is evolving based on the internal and external environment of the group. Just as cultural diversity exists at the individual level, it is argued that issues of diversity also are important to consider at the group level of analysis. Thus, the cultural diversity of groups forms as the culture of the individuals in the groups and the communities in which they grew up and currently live vary. Practitioners have to examine groups from the perspective that although there are many similarities among groups, diversity exists, and practitioners must constantly assess the changes between and within groups and adapt to individual and group needs accordingly.

If one observes a group at a particular point in time, the identity of the group and the functions of the group are dependent on the collective diversity of the membership and the community variables impacting on the group at that moment. Furthermore, open groups (where new members join and others drop out) are subject to continuous change in identities and functions (Yalom, 1985). Levine (1987) also hypothesizes that groups eventually become more homogenous as persons who fit the characteristics of the group become members and those that do not "fit" the group never come or drop out. The social ecological theory of person-environment fit that Levine (1987) and Maton (1989) discuss suggests that over time, group membership characteristics should stabilize to a certain degree. However, as change is inherent to humans and groups, group process and individual needs should constantly fluctuate. Herein lies the challenge for practitioners or resource persons working with mutual assistance groups.

Recommendations for Practitioners

In order to respond to issues of diversity at the individual and group levels, practitioners working with groups must not be passive in their involvement with groups, nor should practitioners presume that they know what is best for the group. Group work requires constant monitoring of practitioners' characteristics and roles with groups. Also, practitioners must utilize strategies that can aid both practitioners' and members' responses to changing group dynamics.

Optimal characteristics of practitioners. In light of the research and theory presented here, group work requires a great deal of flexibility. The constant change occurring at the individual, group, and community levels dictates that a practitioner must constantly respond to these changes. Thus, one cannot sit passively and assume groups are similar and the needs are the same from year to year. The changes that occur require an active participation by practitioners to assess these changes and work to help the members respond to the changes.

In addition to flexibility, practitioners must maintain a keen sense of awareness. Understanding one's own value structure is an important first step to cultural awareness. Observing the values of the groups they serve and the communities in which they live is the next. Examining one's own value system objectively and determining if those values are consistent with or in conflict with that of the group and community at large requires a great deal of insight.

Another important characteristic is sensitivity. Cultural sensitivity is critical to our understanding of individual and group diversity and in many ways encompasses the other characteristics of flexibility and awareness. Cultural diversity at both the individual and group levels has to be acknowledged and observed. The value structure of practitioners and the stereotypes that are formed may affect how one interacts with individuals in the group and how one responds to external factors impinging on the group as a whole. In order to become more sensitive and responsive to cultural diversity, practitioners may choose to participate in workshops or trainings on this issue.

The role of the practitioner. Many professionals play a major role in the early phases of group formation and may be responsible for the group's starting. In this case, the practitioner initially may function as a group leader. However, as groups evolve and develop their own sense of identity, it is ideal if the leadership of the group is transferred to a group member. This enables groups to further develop independent of the practitioner and fosters a greater sense of empowerment within the group.

The concept of member-led groups is central to the philosophy of self-help or mutual assistance groups. Many support groups do not function in this manner and the structure and function of the groups are dictated by an external source, such as the professional facilitator. When this happens, the empowering process of group participation may be undermined, as members defer to professional leaders' ideas and values.

Group strategies. As practitioners function as either leaders or resource persons to groups, several strategies can be employed to help the group respond to the inherent changing dynamics. First, recognizing that most people tend to resist change, educating the membership to the process of change is critical. As membership and goals of the group shift, frequent booster sessions on this topic may be indicated. In this way, members can be reminded that change is expected and that it is necessary and beneficial to change functions or goals of the group in response to changing needs. Helping group members adjust to those changes is the role of the practitioner serving as leader or resource person.

Practitioners can aid group members in their ability to welcome new members and respond appropriately to internal and external influences on the groups. Frequent social functions and team building activities may be helpful. Activities such as these are excellent ice breakers and tend to help members focus on similarities among themselves instead of differences. It then becomes easier for members to work collectively toward common goals and changing functions for the group.

In addition to education, social and team building activities, practitioners can monitor changing needs through formal and informal needs assessment. Practitioners can proactively assess group members' reactions to group process and outcomes. Monitoring how members feel about the structure and function of the group, determining members' satisfaction with group activities, and seeking recommendations for change are critical factors. Frequent needs assessments can be invaluable to the facilitator and leader of the group.

In keeping with the ecological paradigm, multilevel assessments must be conducted periodically (i.e., individual, group, and community assessments). Thus, in addition to gathering information from members, community factors must be assessed, enabling one to remain in touch with community resources and potential barriers and facilitators to group activities. By remaining in touch with changes at the community level, the practitioner can better respond to requests from within the group.

CONCLUSIONS

To foster best practice concepts in group work, group facilitators must follow current research findings in this area and attempt to blend these findings with theory and practice concepts. This paper presented the ecological paradigm as a basis for understanding group dynamics. Following ecological principles, the findings were discussed and it was suggested that issues of diversity and changing needs must be applied to both the individual and group levels of analysis. It is hoped that this discussion will provide a basis for practitioners to begin to think about the principles of ecological theory, issues of diversity at the individual and group levels, and applications to practice with groups.

REFERENCES

Bednar, R., & Kaul, T. (1978). Experiential group research: Current perspectives. In S. Garfield & A. Bergin (Eds.), *Handbook of psychotherapy and behavior change* (2nd ed., pp. 769-815). New York: Basic Books.

Borman, L. (1976). Self-help and the professional. *Social Policy, 7*, 46-47.

Kramer, K., & Nash, K. (1992). Self-help group models: An ecological conceptualization. In A. Katz, H. Hedrick, D. Isenberg, L. Thompson, T. Goodrich, & A. Kutscher (Eds.), *Self help: Concepts and applications* (pp. 144-148). Philadelphia: The Charles Press.

Kurtz, L. (1994). Self-help groups for families with mental illness or alcoholism. In T. Powell (Ed.), *Understanding the self-help organization: Frameworks and findings.* (pp. 293-313). Thousand Oaks, CA: Sage.

Levine, M. (1987, August). *An analysis of mutual assistance.* Invited address, Annual Meeting of the American Psychological Association, New York City.

Levy, L. (1976). Self-help groups: Types and psychological processes. *Journal of Applied Behavioral Science, 12,* 310-322.

Levy, L. (1979). Processes and activities in groups. In M. Lieberman & L. Borman (Eds.), *Self-help groups for coping with crisis* (pp.234-271). San Francisco: Jossey-Bass.

Lipson, J. (1982). Effects of support group on the emotional impact of caesarean childbirth. *Prevention in Human Services, 1,* 17-29.

Luke, D., Roberts, L., & Rappaport, J. (1993). Individual, group context, and individual-group fit predictors of self-help group attendance. *The Journal of Applied Behavioral Science, 29,* 216-238.

Maton, K. (1989). Towards an ecological understanding of mutual-help groups: The social ecology "fit." *American Journal of Community Psychology, 17,* 729-753.

Maton, K. (1993). Moving beyond the individual level of analysis in mutual help group research: An ecological paradigm. *The Journal of Applied Behavioral Science, 29,* 272-286.

Maton, K. (1994). Moving beyond the individual level of analysis in mutual help group research: An ecological paradigm. In T. Powell (Ed.), *Understanding the self-help organization: Frameworks and findings* (pp. 136-153). Thousand Oaks, CA: Sage.

Nash, K., & Kramer, K. (1993). Self-help for sickle cell disease in African-American communities. *The Journal of Applied Behavioral Science, 29,* 202-215.

Nash, K., & Kramer, K. (1994). Self-help for sickle cell disease in African-American communities. In T. Powell (Ed.), *Understanding the self-help organization: Frameworks and findings* (pp. 136-153). Thousand Oaks, CA: Sage.

Schopler, J., & Galinsky, M. (1993). Support groups as open systems: A model for practice and research. *Health & Social Work, 18,* 195-207.

Schubert, M., & Borkman, T. (1994). Identifying the experiential knowledge developed within a self-help group. In T. Powell (Ed.), *Understanding the self-help organization: Frameworks and findings* (pp. 293-313). Thousand Oaks, CA: Sage.

Videka-Sherman, L. (1982). Effects of participation in a self-help group for bereaved parents: Compassionate Friends. *Prevention in Human Services, 1,* 69-77.

Yalom, I. (1985). *The theory and practice of group psychotherapy* (3rd ed.). New York: Basic Books.

Making It Happen:
From Great Idea
to Successful Support Group Program

Carol S. Cohen

SUMMARY. The implementation process of the Grandmothers As Mothers Again support group program serves as a cautionary, yet optimistic tale for practitioners and administrators guiding new programs to institutionalization. Following a review of issues in support group development within a social agency context, the story of GAMA is used to identify four keys to program success. These are: make the program critical, integral, personal, and responsible. *[Single or multiple copies of this article are available from The Haworth Document Delivery Service: 1-800-342-9678, 9:00 a.m. - 5:00 p.m. (EST).]*

With the words, "Son, this is important!", a delegation of grandmothers requested agency assistance in convening a support group for women facing parenthood for the second time. Considering this beginning, it may shock some that it took two years for the GAMA

Carol S. Cohen, DSW, is Assistant Professor, Fordham University Graduate School of Social Service, 113 West 60 Street, New York, NY 10023.

The author acknowledges the ongoing work of Catholic Charities, Diocese of Brooklyn in creating and supporting the GAMA program.

This paper was developed from a presentation by Carol Cohen, Marianne Chierchio, Phyllis Lee Krauser, and Ruth Francis at the XV Annual Symposium, Association for the Advancement of Social Work with Groups, October 1993, New York.

67

(Grandmothers As Mothers Again) support group program to reach solid implementation, and that none of the original clients partici-pated beyond their initial request. On the other hand, considering the exigencies of agency and community life, it may surprise others that it began at all. The evolution of the GAMA program illustrates some of the common difficulties in developing an effective support group program. GAMA's story and analysis addresses the concerns of workers, supervisors, and administrators, who are worried about "making it happen."

REVIEW OF FACTORS IN SUPPORT GROUP IMPLEMENTATION

During the last twenty years, many agencies have adopted the attitude of: "Groups Don't Work Here" (Cohen, 1993). They arrive at this juncture after witnessing great idea after great idea aban-doned before successful implementation. A review of the literature points to several factors that contribute to group implementation failures, including lack of complementarity of group goals and methods with agency context; incomplete staff negotiation through each stage of implementation; insufficient attention to planning before groups begin meeting; and diminution of professional com-petence in leading and supervising group programs.

The failure to consider the degree of synchronization of the goals and methodology of the group program with the mission and func-tion of the agency setting often places group programs outside of the "real" work of the agency (Garland, 1992). The literature sug-gests that social workers contemplating support group programs carefully assess the agency's ideology about groups (Cohen, 1994), and then design a complementary structure. When groups are seen as "frills" (Kurland, Getzel, & Salmon, 1986), they are often early failures or the first programs to be abandoned during times of agency constriction.

Although support group programs can forge new areas of service delivery, they need to be presented and nurtured with an under-standing of formal and informal agency structures (Gitterman, 1986). Gilbert's (1989) case study of a support group in a health setting illustrates the need for careful initial agency assessment, as well as for political negotiation through each phase of the implementation process. Utilizing a biological metaphor, Hasenfeld and Schmid (1989) suggest that the agency needs and skills used by administrators must shift as agencies move through their life cycle. Advocates for support group programs must similarly adapt and utilize strategies that are appropriately tied to the stage of agency and program development. Incomplete political negotiation within the agency context during any stage of the implementation process (Patti, 1983) appears to stunt the development of group programs.

Inattention to the planning of groups before they meet has been identified as a source of program failure (Kurland, 1978). Garland (1992) mentions the common phrase of "doing a group," and asks if social workers would use the expression "doing a client?" His question is quite useful to raise consciousness about the need to approach a group intervention in a respectful manner, and implies that workers often neglect the critical area of planning and program design.

The decreased emphasis over the last twenty years in graduate social work education on practice with groups (Meyer, 1986) has led to fewer professionals who can plan and implement group programs, as well as fewer social workers who see social group work approaches as effective responses to client needs. Even when social workers work with groups, they rarely credit their graduate education as their base of knowledge in this area (Birnbaum, Middleman, & Huber, 1989). With lack of exposure, social worker ambivalence towards group formation is seen as normative in agency practice (Kurland & Salmon, 1989).

All of these factors have affected the Grandmothers As Mothers Again program. As the story of GAMA shows, the program survived a difficult beginning and became institutionalized through the combination of four key ingredients. GAMA's example lends support to the work of others in this field, and advances the discussion by suggesting a new conceptualization of the key ingredients needed to build a successful support group program.

THE STORY OF GAMA

Today, two GAMA groups meet biweekly, one operating in English and the other in Spanish. Members have assumed their parenting roles through a variety of events, including their children's deaths from AIDS, incarceration, substance abuse, and abandonment. The members of the Spanish-speaking GAMA group are Latinas, originally from the Caribbean and Central America. Members of the English-speaking group are African-American and African-Caribbean. All the ethnic groups represented in the membership have a cultural history of caring for grandchildren through extended family networks, but the members' current arrangements represent a dramatic departure, due to the devastating nature of the events leading the grandmothers to take on parental responsibilities.

According to the United States census (1991), 3.2 million children under 18 live with their grandparents, representing an almost 40% increase in the last ten years. GAMA members' new caretaking roles have resulted in the re-alignment of family structures, often accompanied by shattered dreams and economic hardship. As the members quickly note, there are unexpected joys and benefits associated with their new responsibilities, including renewed vigor and interests. All members express love and concern for their grandchildren. Yet, they are equally clear that the assumption of "second time mothering" has been a difficult transition at best. As corroborated in the study of African American grandmothers in Oakland, California (Minkler & Roe, 1993), the failure of their own children to serve as primary caretakers because of absence, incapacity, or refusal is often a source of anger, guilt, and shame to these grandmothers.

The GAMA program is now an integrated part of a multi-service unit of a large voluntary agency in New York City. GAMA's work is focused on sharing the burdens and blessings of the members' situations, through discussion and activity. Workers facilitate discussions, help members plan group content, bring in outside resources to the group, and provide advocacy and crisis services to individual members as needed. In keeping with Schwartz's (1971, p. 7) definition of a social work group, GAMA is "a collection of people, who need each other in order to work on certain tasks, in an agency hospitable to those tasks." The powerful impact of the group is seen in the words of members, who report: "I'm not isolated anymore"; "We all share the same problem"; and "When I give help I feel better."

With professional leadership, GAMA has become a support group. The efforts of GAMA's members and workers provide benefits of "greater social resources, increased knowledge about the concern that members share, a sense of relief and reassurance, and enhanced skills for coping with their situation" (Schopler & Galinsky, 1993, p. 201). Because of the members' key roles in shaping the group, GAMA's purposes encompass the major components of self-help groups: (1) eliminating isolation; (2) gaining perspective; and (3) developing a sense of empowerment (Kirkland, 1992).

The initial idea for the program was greeted with great staff enthusiasm. The unit administrator assigned the supervisor to coordinate the project with a social worker and student intern as co-leaders of the group. As the unit administrator reported: "I loved the idea of grandmothers approaching the staff member and requesting a group." The supervisor (the author), had been hoping for an opportunity like this, and exclaimed, "Finally–A Group!" As co-leaders, the worker and student began outreach efforts after determining the meeting place (at the site of the original request for service) and a schedule of bi-monthly meetings. They mailed invitations to the clients making the initial request; with the supervisor, they planned for a first meeting in which those requesting the service would form the purpose and structure of the group. As planning continued, reports from staff indicated optimism and investment, such as the administrator's expectation of an "easy time" and the excitement throughout the planning process of the co-leaders.

The first meeting took place in January, 1992, with five grandmothers and two leaders in attendance. The group leaders and members introduced themselves, followed by an invitation to the members to frame the purpose of the group. As the leaders discovered, no grandmothers who originally requested the group were present. When participants were asked why they were present, they stated that they had come to the center for a particular reason (either food package, soup kitchen meal, information on services, and/or entitlement advocacy), and were informed that they should attend the group for grandmothers beginning in a few minutes. The leaders engaged those present in approving the bi-monthly schedule, and led a discussion of group purpose and structure. They proposed the

GAMA name for the group and it was unanimously approved. The reactions of staff at this juncture reflected continued excitement, tempered by concern about the odd attendance pattern.

GAMA meetings were held bimonthly from January to June, 1992. The attendance was very poor, with one to four participants. One grandmother consistently attended, while others came once and did not return. The supervisor and co-leaders met between sessions and discussed the progress and plan for the group, using process recordings of the sessions. The unit administrator and group leaders frequently raised the idea of expanding the recruitment base to any grandmother (regardless of caretaking roles), but after extensive discussion, a reluctant agreement was reached to limit membership to grandmothers acting as parents.

At the same time that the group was "failing," interest in grandmothers raising grandchildren was rising. In the national press, the cover story of *U.S. News and World Report* of December 1991 was "Grandparents, the Silent Saviors" (1991). In the professional arena, the March 1992 issue of *NASW News* contained an article about "Second-Time-Around Families" (Landers, 1992); the Brookdale Grandparent Caregiver Information Project (Driver, 1992) was founded in Berkeley, California; AARP (1993) announced the formation of the Grandparent Information Center; and the New York City Department of Health and the Department for the Aging jointly sponsored a conference on grandparent caregivers, and disseminated the report: "Grandparents as Parents of Last Resort" (Brouard & Joslin, 1991). It appeared that the idea of groups such as GAMA (if not the actual progress of the group) captured the imagination of the public and the profession, as well as the agency. Top-level agency managers had heard about the group from the unit administrator, and began to use the concept of the group in fundraising and public relations materials.

The staff team looked for new recruitment strategies, analyzed the poor attendance, and in general, worked to overcome the sense of despair. The leaders posted flyers in the local church and senior centers, as well as telephoned and mailed invitations to single session attendees. In late spring, the supervisor began a group work seminar for agency staff, including the worker assigned to the group. By July 1992, increasing staff disillusionment was evident as

GAMA recessed for the summer, with some hope of renewed effort in the fall. Following the departure of the student intern in May, and the supervisor in August, the primary coordination and supervision of the program fell to the administrator. At the end of the summer, the one consistent GAMA member informed the worker that she was pregnant and would not be returning to the group. The decision was made not to continue the group at that site.

During the months from September 1992-January 1993, GAMA meetings were put on hold while other work continued. The former supervisor consulted with the remaining team members and together they extracted lessons from the first year's experience and worked through feelings of failure. With the addition of a newly hired social worker as a co-leader, and the gift of hindsight, the team took another look at the intensity of participant's disclosures at the first (and last) meeting they attended. Using process recordings of the sessions, it appeared that the leaders and one regular member encouraged a "spilling" pattern since it seemed so therapeutic and exciting. With low attendance, it seemed reasonable at the time to focus the most attention on new participants and their stories, but this early disclosure pattern was counterproductive to the group's development.

Team members reflected on their investment in the project, and noted points of personal resonance. In particular, the new worker pointed out that she had been raised by her grandmother, reminding the team that the other worker shared this history as well. The administrator agreed to keep options for GAMA open, by not redirecting the workers' attention to another large on-going project.

The administrator continued to cite GAMA as a program of the unit, and was encouraged by positive feedback in every forum in which it was mentioned. In January 1993, she and the new worker attended a community forum to speak about agency services. When they mentioned the GAMA program the usual enthusiasm was joined by two offers of collaboration. In the first, the pastor of a predominantly Latino parish stated that he had many parishioners who met the GAMA criteria, and suggested starting a Spanish-speaking group at the church. In the second offer, a child welfare agency in an adjoining neighborhood offered to recruit members and a settlement house agreed to provide meeting space.

This exciting news was brought to the next staff meeting and workers began preparations. Following further negotiations with the collaborators, the new groups began in February and March 1993. Both workers attended the first meetings, but each was assigned primary leadership responsibility of one group. Although the unit administrator's cautious statement, "time will tell" was realistic, the workers reported that the groups were off to a good start.

By May 1993 both groups had been meeting regularly with a core membership of five to ten members. The groups met together for a bilingual Mothers Day celebration, with members contributing refreshments. As the workers reported, everyone was on "cloud nine." The staff witnessed their hard work rewarded, and the members enjoyed the celebration and recognition. Group activities included a game of acting out scenes from childhood, such as playing tag and modeling new clothes. Towards the end of the event, one member volunteered that she was the first to call and join GAMA and has since learned to appreciate and enjoy her granddaughter more. She proudly reported being chosen for a special training program by the Housing Authority. Another member said she felt relieved now that she is connected with the child welfare agency working with GAMA, and can better help her granddaughter deal with the loss of her mother and the death of her grandfather, the member's husband. At this, a member shared that she had been a client of the child welfare agency for several years and that they had been helpful. Another member commented that with GAMA, "I found a place where I could find support – with mothers like me that can understand my hurt." At the end, a member thanked the group and related the strength she derives from God. After asking the group's permission, she sang a special song of thanks.

Following this high point, GAMA moved into a stage of organizational maturity and continued to institutionalization as a key agency service. From June 1993 through the present, the integration of new members has focused attention back to the purpose of the group as well as to deeper areas for work. For example, a new member joined in October 1993, and listened, holding back tears, as three grandmothers related the reasons they cared for their grandchildren and great-grandchildren. The new member then told the group that she did not want to make the same mistakes with her grandchild that she did with her own girls. The group welcomed her and sharing her worries, suggested that they invite a speaker to talk with the group about the development of children. Enhanced group cohesion accompanied the shift from extended revelations to sharing common experiences.

GAMA's content has become more diversified as members have expanded their role in planning. The members discussed fundraising after deciding to begin social outings as a part of GAMA, and with the assistance of a social work intern, decorated and sold tee shirts with a GAMA logo. Currently, the members and staff are working with the New York City Department for the Aging to create a child-care respite program that will serve as a model for future endeavors.

The agency unit has resisted pressure to replicate the group on a much larger scale, although it is negotiating to form an additional group in another section of Brooklyn. Ironically, this group might engage the initial clients requesting the service. After 18 months, they re-appeared at the community office and asked, "What happened to our group?" The worker finally discovered that he had misinterpreted them when they said they lived in the "projects," thinking they meant the buildings across the street. In fact, they lived in Housing Authority buildings a few miles away and rarely ventured to the neighborhood where the community office is located.

Invitations to speak about GAMA in agency and community forums have increased; discussion about grandparents raising grandchildren has continued to expand in both the popular and professional press (Cantor & Brennan, 1993; Kutner, 1994: Young, 1993). The intense interest and positive feedback has challenged the administrator and co-leaders to continually focus on GAMA's central core: the mutual aid among members. In a poignant illustration, group members were engaged in planning strategies for member recruitment. The members decided to create their own flyer, including the message, "We know you need support and we're here for you."

THE LESSONS OF GAMA

The ultimate survival of Grandmothers As Mothers Again suggests that the following four key ingredients were in place and activated to sustain it through difficult times. In effect, these elements enabled staff to maximize opportunities and to minimize problems.

Making it critical. Grandmothers raising grandchildren have cited support by those in similar situations as one of their most important needs and most effective resources (Brookdale, 1993; Kirkland, 1993; Minkler & Roe, 1993; Young, 1993). Even when despairing, staff continually acknowledged the value of the support these women could provide to each other. In its first year, GAMA sometimes lost this purpose, and often took on a therapeutic and individualized, remedial focus. The redirection of workers' attention back to "support" from "healing" helped the program back on track.

Grandmothers have additional needs beyond social support, and the group's flexibility in accommodating those needs and finding outside resources when needed was important to its success. The worker linked members with the agency's full range of entitlement, counseling, health, and educational services outside the meetings, and incorporated respite, socialization, and information gathering within the meetings themselves. GAMA was a project worth continuing, critical to the population it was designed to serve.

Making it integral. As noted earlier (Garland, 1992; Gilbert, 1989; Gitterman, 1986), one of the most frequently cited reasons for implementation failure is the lack of integration of groups with the larger organization. In GAMA's case, the overall mission of the agency is conceived as "building caring communities" and "helping the most vulnerable." GAMA reaches out to a highly vulnerable population, seeking to build community among peers and strengthen devastated families. GAMA's purposes of eliminating isolation through mutual aid, increasing knowledge and sense of perspective, and developing a sense of empowerment affords the opportunity for integration within the larger agency context. The unit administrator and supervisor capitalized on this, speaking about GAMA with staff from other agency units, and allocating and sustaining a large amount of staff time to this project. GAMA linked the unit's commitment to the greater commitment of the agency.

Early identification of barriers to GAMA's success, especially the lack of workers' skill in group work practice was helpful. This was brought to the agency's attention with a proposal for enhancing skills with groups in many units of the agency. When problems are identified they are generally less threatening to the status quo of organizations when solutions are suggested at the same time (Kingdon, 1984), and the supervisor was encouraged to proceed with the agency-wide training program. The supervisor saw herself as a human services entrepreneur and "idea manager" (Tropman, 1989), whose task was to solidly integrate GAMA into the overall agency and unit structure.

This high degree of integration may have saved the program when abandonment seemed prudent, since the administrator would have had to account for its demise. Regular team meetings, the use of process recordings, and the inclusion of multiple staff members in the planning and implementation process, built a sense of ownership and promoted the view of GAMA as the "type of program the agency should be doing."

Making it personal. The personal stakes of staff are always present, and can become a source of goal displacement (Perrow, 1986). When acknowledged and marshaled effectively, they can fuel a project that is difficult and rife with disappointment. GAMA's story suggests that all of the principal staff members had some kind of personal connection to the project, beyond the necessary commitment to serve clients effectively. The two current workers were primarily raised by their grandmothers. Their history provided them a legacy of personal experience to draw on and an affinity for each other that bridged the cultural and racial differences among the group participants. Both reported feeling a spiritual re-connection with their grandmothers through their work with the group. Attention to supervision and training insured that countertransference did not damage the group process, and the personal connection of the workers to GAMA may help explain the workers' ability to sustain their commitment to the group.

The personal connections of the supervisor (later serving as consultant) and unit administrator to the GAMA program were less surprising, but still powerful. The supervisor saw GAMA as one of her last opportunities to institutionalize group work practice in the agency network of service modalities. The administrator recognized the advantages of framing the work of her program in the context of the agency mission. The unit was seen as creative, but well within agency boundaries. Further, by taking a proactive stance in program design, she was able to maintain more control over the deployment of staff when faced with agency-wide mandates for service.

Making it responsible. Responsibility in program design and implementation involves the recognition that clients' lives can be deeply affected by support group programs. The two areas of greatest concern were for ongoing staff supervision and training. Reserving time was difficult, but the team members committed themselves to a regular series of meetings to discuss the group. When the needs for skill development proved too great to be covered in supervision, the idea for the group work seminar was generated and instituted. The seminar normalized the lack of exposure and skill with groups among the participants, and focused on the essential areas of group dynamics and interventions (Schopler & Galinsky, 1993). In addition, the seminar enabled the participating worker to see GAMA as a field for learning, rather that as a failing effort. The staff was challenged to provide the highest quality of service possible; this duty often required painful scrutiny of practice and a determination to follow a purposive planning process for and with the group.

The staff shifted gears as the project moved through its stages of development (Hasenfeld & Schmid, 1989). The administrator continued to gather resources and advance the idea of the group; in later stages, she also began to protect the project from inappropriate expansion that might deleteriously alter its essential core. The supervisor moved with the needs of the group and the workers, and even after leaving the agency, continued to provide ongoing consultation and training. The workers made the transition from trying to find solutions, to enabling the members to help each other. In its later stages, they helped the group build a model of democratic decision making that has resulted in accomplishing the group's purpose and in taking members into new and exciting areas of work.

CONCLUSIONS

The story of the Grandmothers As Mothers support group serves as a cautionary, yet optimistic, tale for practitioners and administrators guiding new programs to institutionalization. In its present stage of development, it is hard to imagine that the GAMA program was ever in jeopardy, yet it faced abandonment at many points. The intensity of potential members' needs, the goodness of fit with agency mission, the healthy self interest of involved staff, and the commitment to professional service contributed to the programs survival. These ingredients, making the program critical, integral, personal, and responsible, nourished GAMA and allowed it to thrive.

REFERENCES

American Association of Retired Persons (1993). *Grandparents raising their grandchildren.* Washington D.C.: AARP Grandparent Information Center.

Birnbaum, M. L., Middleman, R. R., & Huber, R. (1989, October). *Where social workers obtain their knowledge base in group work.* Paper presented at the Annual Meeting of the National Association of Social Workers, San Francisco, CA.

Brouard, A. & Joslin, D. (1991). *Grandparents as parents of last resort: A survey of three department of health child health clinics.* New York: City of New York Department of Health and Department for the Aging.

Cantor, M. & Brennan, M. (1993). *Growing older in New York City in the 1990's; Volume 5: Family and community support systems of older New Yorkers.* New York: The New York Center for Policy on Aging of the New York Community Trust.

Cohen, C. S. (1994, March). *Promoting multi-method field instruction: Assessment and action framework.* Paper presented March, 1994 at the Council on Social Work Education Annual Program Meeting, Atlanta, GA.

Cohen, C. S. (1993). Enhancing social group work opportunities in field work education. *Dissertation Abstracts International, 54* (01), 317A. (University Microfilms No. 9315454).

Driver, D. (1992). *Brookdale Grandparent Caregiver Information Project Newsletter, 1*(1).

Garland, J. (1992). Developing and sustaining group work services: A systemic and systematic view. *Social Work with Groups, 15* (4), 89-98.

Gilbert, C. M. (1989). Developing a group program in a health care setting. *Social Work with Groups, 12* (4), 27-43.

Gitterman, A. (1986). Developing a new group service. In A. Gitterman & L. Shulman (Eds.), *Mutual aid groups and the life cycle* (pp. 53-71). Itasca, IL: F. E. Peacock.

Hasenfeld, Y. & Schmid, H. (1989). The life cycle of human service organizations: An administrative perspective. *Administration in Social Work, 13* (3/4), 243-269.

Kingdon, J. W. (1984). *Agenda, alternatives and public policies.* Boston: Little Brown and Co.

Kirkland, B. (1992, February). Definition of a self-help group. *Grandparents United Newsletter,* p. 1.

Kurland, R. (1978). Planning: The neglected component of group development. *Social Work with Groups, 1* (2), 173-178.

Kurland, R. & Salmon, R. (1989). Concentrations and methods: Combining core content and specialized expertise in the teaching of group work. *Journal of Teaching in Social Work, 3*(1), 87-99.

Kurland, R., Getzel, G., & Salmon, R. (1986). Sowing groups in infertile fields: Curriculum and other strategies to overcome resistance to the formation of new groups. In M. Parnes (Ed.), *Innovations in social group work: Feedback from practice to theory, Proceedings of the annual group work symposium* (pp. 57-74). New York: The Haworth Press, Inc.

Kutner, L. (1994, April 7). Parent & child. *The New York Times.* p. C12.

Landers, S. (1992, March). "Second-time-around families" find aid. *NASW News,* p. 5.

Meyer, C. (1986). *Curriculum policy statements in social work education. #6, Social work education monograph series.* Austin: School of Social Work, The University of Texas at Austin.

Minkler, M. & Roe, K. M. (1993). *Grandmothers as caregivers.* Newbury Park, CA: Sage Publications, Inc.

Patti, R. J. (1983). *Social welfare administration: Managing social programs in a developmental context.* Englewood Cliffs, N.J.: Prentice Hall.

Perrow, C. (1986). *Complex organizations* (3rd ed.). New York: Random House.

Schopler, J. H. & Galinsky, M. J. (1993). Support groups as open systems: A model for practice and research. *Health and Social Work, 18* (3), 195- 207.

Schwartz, W. (1971). On the use of groups in social work practice. In W. Schwartz & S. Zalba (Eds.), *The practice of group work* (pp. 3-24). New York: Columbia University Press.

Tropman, J. E. (1989). Human service entrepreneurship: The four "C" approach. *Administration in Social Work, 13* (3/4), 219-242.

U.S. Bureau of the Census (1991). *Current population reports: Marital status and living arrangements* (Series P-20, No. 450). Washington, D.C.: Government Printing Office.

Young, J. (1993, September 7). It isn't easy to parent again. *Daily News,* p. 4-KSI.

My Partner Is Hurting:
Group Work with Male Partners
of Adult Survivors of Sexual Abuse

Kenneth Reid
Gary Mathews
Peggy Solow Liss

SUMMARY. Male adult survivors of childhood sexual abuse, as well as male partners of survivors often experience problems. There are few service alternatives available to them. One innovative program combines both populations in a two-group sequence. The first group is time-limited. Members graduate to a second, open-ended group. The innovative elements of these sequenced support groups include the concept of secondary victim, the combination of male partners with male survivors, sequenced time-limited and ongoing groups, and the use of mixed gender leaders with same-sex groups. *[Single or multiple copies of this article are available from The Haworth Document Delivery Service: 1-800-342-9678, 9:00 a.m. - 5:00 p.m. (EST).]*

When male partners of sexually abused women and gay men need counseling services, where do they turn? This description of a

Kenneth Reid, PhD, and Gary Mathews, PhD, are Professors in the School of Social Work at Western Michigan University, Kalamazoo, MI 49008. Peggy Solow Liss, MSW, is Clinical Consultant to the Sexual Assault Program, YWCA Kalamazoo, 353 East Michigan, Kalamazoo, MI 49007-3844.

[Haworth co-indexing entry note]: "My Partner Is Hurting: Group Work with Male Partners of Adult Survivors of Sexual Abuse." Reid, Kenneth, Gary Mathews, and Peggy Solow Liss. Co-published simultaneously in *Social Work with Groups* (The Haworth Press, Inc.) Vol. 18, No. 1, 1995, pp. 81-87; and: *Support Groups: Current Perspectives on Theory and Practice* (ed: Maeda J. Galinsky, and Janice H. Schopler) The Haworth Press, Inc., 1995, pp. 81-87. Single or multiple copies of this article are available from The Haworth Document Delivery Center [1-800-342-9678, 9:00 a.m. - 5:00 p.m. (EST)].

support group for male partners of adult survivors examines one alternative. Data is taken from the records and experiences of men's groups sponsored by the YWCA Sexual Assault Program (Y-SAP), in Kalamazoo, Michigan. The systemic impact of sexual abuse on significant others is acknowledged in the logic of the program design.

The program is founded on the previous experiences of similar groups with the survivors themselves that have been reported in the literature. Group therapy has been established as a legitimate modality for serving survivors of sexual abuse. Support groups (Gil, 1990) and clinical groups (Cole, 1985; Draucker, 1992) have both proven successful. The various formats run the gamut from closed, structured, and time-limited (Bruckner and Johnson, 1987; Goodman and Nowak-Scibelli, 1985; Gordy, 1983) to open, unstructured and ongoing (Blake-White and Kline, 1985). Sgroi (1989b) described survivors groups combining elements of both time-limited and ongoing formats by offering three time-limited groups each year and permitting survivors to cycle through them as many as three times.

Even though the group program described is founded on previous work, there are some new concepts of note. They include the concept of secondary victim, the combination of male partners of survivors with male survivors, sequenced time-limited and ongoing groups, and the use of mixed gender leaders with same-sex groups. The secondary victim is mostly overlooked in the literature. The combination of members who are partners with members who are survivors facilitates seeing the problem from another's perspective without the emotional charge present in discussions with one's own partner. The sequencing of the groups provides choice for the participant, the potential for rapid progress in the initial time-limited group, and continuity for the on-going group. The same-sex composition of the membership acknowledges the sensitive content of discussions. The mixed gender leadership permits modeling.

At the Kalamazoo, Michigan Young Women's Christian Association Sexual Assault Program (Y-SAP), two sequential groups for men are offered. The first group is a time-limited one, eight weeks in length. When participants "graduate" from the initial group, they are eligible for membership in the ongoing group. These groups help men to understand, accept, and eventually get beyond the disclosure of their own or their partner's childhood sexual abuse.

Informing a partner of abuse is difficult and risky. Some survivors therefore decide not to tell partners until late in the flowering of the relationship. Partners, having learned of the survivor's sexual abuse history, often feel unprepared, shocked, and unsure. According to Maltz (1991), couples tend to stop communicating: One partner may withdraw emotionally; one partner may fail to involve the other partner in the healing process; or, one partner may be uncooperative. These problems make the partner a likely candidate for a support group.

DESCRIPTION OF THE TWO TYPES OF GROUPS

Utilizing the framework developed by Schopler and Galinsky (1993) the two types of groups for partners and survivors will be described in relation to the dimensions of environment, group characteristics, group conditions, and outcomes.

Environmental conditions. Potential members for the initial, time-limited group are referred by the such diverse sources as Y-SAP caseworkers, counseling agencies, and client word of mouth. The sponsor is Y-SAP. The idea originated from their group for women who are survivors of sexual abuse. Leaders are drawn from a combination of in-house staff and part-time staff recruited from the local university. Recruitment and screening for the initial group is handled by the Y-SAP staff. These groups for partners and survivors are segregated by sex (Fedele and Harrington, 1990). Entrance to the ongoing group is limited to "graduates" of the time-limited group, and occurs immediately following the termination of the initial group. Members exhibiting difficulty in adjusting to the norms of the initial group either withdraw prior to completion of the original group, or are informed they should not continue.

Participant characteristics. Although membership is limited to males, each group is co-led by a male-female team. Mixed gender leadership teams have been reported in both women's support groups and a male survivors group (Bruckner and Johnson, 1987). One reason for this is the opportunity to model healthy, positive, mutually respectful female-male relationships to the members. A female "sounding board" is available. Initial reaction to a female leader has varied widely, from pleasant surprise to indifference to "either she goes or I go." With rare exceptions, members eventually accept the presence and contributions of a female leader.

The number of members is limited to twelve in the initial group. The same is theoretically true for the open-ended group, although it has never reached maximum capacity. The attrition in the initial group is usually one to three members. The ongoing group has five or six core members, with several additional persons attending sporadically, or attending for several meetings immediately following the termination of the initial group and then dropping out.

Participants vary in age from early twenties to late sixties. The men include the unemployed, craftsmen, custodians, and professionals. Some are married, some divorced, some are living with female partners, and some with male partners. The composition has included European Americans and African Americans, so the groups are diverse in age, race and class.

Leadership must be provided by experienced and skilled professionals. Expert knowledge of support groups and sexual abuse is required, together with an ability to gently confront the members. The presence of professionally trained leaders distinguishes this group from many other support groups.

Group conditions. The Y-SAP organized its first support group for male partners and survivors in 1990. The goals of the sequential time-limited and open-ended groups are to educate the men about childhood sexual abuse and victimization; to provide opportunity to ventilate and clarify feelings in a confidential setting; to receive support from other men in similar circumstances, thus reducing a commonly reported sense of isolation; and to teach ways of being supportive to their present or future partners. The themes discussed include the dynamics of sexual abuse, anger, isolation, sexual problems such as promiscuity and low sexual desire, and powerlessness. The felicitous combination of partners and survivors in the same group is a fascinating and often fruitful opportunity for them to exchange perspectives.

Two short-term groups are offered during each calendar year, and each meets weekly for an hour and a half in the evening. The ongoing group meets twice monthly. A member of the ongoing group is sometimes invited to attend one of the final sessions of the introductory group to personally invite participants to attend the ongoing group.

Outcomes and practice implications. Partners of survivors are secondary victims of abuse. Partners experience problems deserving attention on their own merits, not just to better support their mates who are the primary victims. Combining survivors of all types of abuse has been reported in the literature (Gil, 1990), but this is believed to be the first reported instance of same-gender support groups for partners and survivors. The outcomes and practice implications discussed below are based on the experience of the group leaders, the self-reports of participants, and the supporting literature cited throughout this report. The verbal feedback elicited during each termination session of the time-limited group has been particularly informative.

Dramatic and rapid progress often occurs in the initial group. New participants unanimously report coming to the first session with a sense of isolation resulting from the stigma attached to the subject of sexual abuse. The usual sources of social support are frequently not utilized for this most private of subjects. Self-disclosure often occurs rapidly in the group, and the leaders' early challenge is to modulate the pace rather than to draw out reluctant members of the group. There are usually a few withdrawn members, but they are exposed to the modeling of those that discuss their situations without prompting, thus setting a normative climate of active participation. These gains are reinforced and maintained in the ongoing group.

On the negative side, many men come to this group as a last hope. If they fail here, the disappointment can be profound. Because the wounds are sometimes deep, because the plight of the secondary victim is partially dependent on the progress of the primary victim, and because the presenting symptoms can be multiple and severe, it is inevitable that sometimes men drop out, or finish the group with a feeling of dashed hopes.

The men must occasionally be admonished against blaming their partners, the primary victims. Partners tend to express commitment to the survivor's healing, but there is frequent frustration and dissatisfaction expressed toward the present state of their relationships.

When the relationship is with a female partner, the tone of the discussion can degenerate into female bashing, an exaggerated and stereotypical expression of anger toward women in general. The presence of a female co-leader moderates this tendency, as does the presence of survivors.

The support group provides men with a structured, safe opportunity to obtain information, support, and to express strong, previously repressed feelings. It also gives men the chance to help and support others. A discussion of shared problems with brittle, unstable, sexually frustrating relationships is an inevitable part of every group session. Failed relationships, serial liaisons and promiscuity are common. The benefit for partners is the opportunity to hear familiar themes and concerns expressed by the survivors in the group, without the emotional baggage of their own partners. The benefit for survivors is to hear the partners in the group experiencing the same frustrations and struggles as their own partners. In other words, they are sharing the common benefits of empathy, universalization, self-disclosure, and modeling, but they are bringing to the group experience the unique points of view of their respective role relationships.

While no outcome study has been performed with the participants in these uniquely sequenced groups, the word of mouth referrals from previous group participants, and the continued strong demand for the initial groups are indicators of success. The verbal feedback elicited during each termination session of the initial group is positive.

The behavioral, cognitive, or affective changes that can be accomplished in a support group experience are limited in extent. The number of long term participants in the ongoing group is small. The men are, however, exposed to accurate information about the nature of sexual abuse. They are provided an opportunity to discuss openly a pressing problem with competent professionals and other men in similar situations. They experience the universalization of their previously self-isolating experience. And they know that an ongoing group experience is available should they choose to avail themselves. This is one method of helping partners of survivors and survivors to begin to break the cycle of isolation, pain, and anger.

REFERENCES

Blake-White, J. and Kline, C.M. (1985). Treating the dissociative process in adult victims of childhood incest. *Social Casework: The Journal of Contemporary Social Work,* 66, 394-402.

Bruckner, D.F. and Johnson, P.E. (1987). Treatment for adult male victims of childhood sexual abuse. *Social Casework: The Journal of Contemporary Social Work,* 68, 81-87.

Cole, C.L. (1985). A group design for adult female survivors of childhood incest. *Women and Therapy,* 4(3), 71-82.

Draucker, C.B. (1992). *Counseling survivors of childhood sexual abuse.* London: Sage Publications.

Fedele, N.M. and Harrington, E.A. (1990). Women's groups: How connections heal. *Work in Progress,* Occasional Publication of The Stone Center, *No 47* pp. 1-12),Wellesley, MA: Wellesley College.

Gil, E. (1990). *Treatment of adult survivors of childhood sexual abuse.* Walnut Creek, CA: Launch.

Goodman, B. and Nowak-Scibelli, D. (1985). Group treatment for women incestuously abused as children. *International Journal of Group Psychotherapy,* 35, 531-544.

Gordy, P.L. (1983). Group work that supports adult victims of childhood incest. *Social Casework: The Journal of Contemporary Social Work,* 64, 300-307.

Maltz, W. (1991). *The sexual healing journey: A guide for survivors of sexual abuse.* New York: Harper Collins.

Schopler, J.H. and Galinsky, M.J. (1983). Support groups as open systems: A model for practice and research. *Health & Social Work,* 18(3), 195-207.

Sgroi, S.M. (1989b). Healing together: Peer group therapy for adult survivors of child sexual abuse. In S.M. Sgroi (Ed.), *Vulnerable populations: Vol. 2 Sexual abuse treatment for children, adult survivors, and persons with mental retardation* (pp. 131-166), Lexington, MA: Lexington Books.

A Support Group for Families
of Armed Services Personnel
in the Persian Gulf War

Sam Parker
Duncan Hutchinson
Stephanie Berry

SUMMARY. During the Persian Gulf War, the Red Cross and a family service agency in Greensboro, North Carolina, began a multi-generational support group designed to serve military families. The major features of this innovative group approach are described in relation to the major dimensions of Schopler and Galinsky's (1993) model of support groups. From this group experience, the leaders learned the significance of appropriate sponsorship in providing an appealing environment, the importance of inclusiveness, a greater understanding of the enrichment that diversity brings, and the significance of the role that mentor families can play in a support group. *[Single or multiple copies of this article are available from The Haworth Document Delivery Service: 1-800-342-9678, 9:00 a.m. - 5:00 p.m. (EST).]*

Sam Parker, ACSW, is Director of Professional Services, Family and Children's Service, 301 East Washington Street, Greensboro, NC 27401. Duncan Hutchinson, BS, is Director of Emergency Services, Greensboro Chapter, American Red Cross, 1100 North Church Street, Greensboro, NC 27401. Stephanie Berry, BA, is Student Intern, Family and Children's Service, 301 East Washington Street, Greensboro, NC 27401.

[Haworth co-indexing entry note]: "A Support Group for Families of Armed Services Personnel in the Persian Gulf War." Parker, Sam, Duncan Hutchinson, and Stephanie Berry. Co-published simultaneously in *Social Work with Groups* (The Haworth Press, Inc.) Vol. 18, No. 1, 1995, pp. 89-97; and: *Support Groups: Current Perspectives on Theory and Practice* (ed: Maeda J. Galinsky, and Janice H. Schopler) The Haworth Press, Inc., 1995, pp. 89-97. Single or multiple copies of this article are available from The Haworth Document Delivery Center [1-800-342-9678, 9:00 a.m. - 5:00 p.m. (EST)].

89

THE CRISIS

In October of 1990, two agencies in Greensboro, North Carolina, joined together in an effort to serve military families directly affected by the Persian Gulf War. The Red Cross, with its mission to serve military families, and Family and Children's Service, with its mission to strengthen families, planned and carried out a support group designed to help families of armed services personnel deployed to the Gulf. This group was defined as a support group because its primary focus was to facilitate mutual help among people dealing with the common crisis of having a family member in an overseas war. Professional leadership was provided by a social worker and a pastoral counselor.

A review of the literature (Kleiger, Kennedy, Becker, & Smith, 1993; Schopler & Galinsky, 1993; Schwartzben, 1989; Stewart et al., 1992; Wadsworth, 1993) indicates that this was an innovative group intervention. The nature of the collaboration between agencies was one novel feature of this support group. This group was also unusual in that it was very inclusive. It targeted not only spouses of armed services personnel but also the entire family system, and managed to attract and keep a membership that was remarkably diverse. Yet another unusual feature of this group was the decision to include in the group several veterans (and spouses) of earlier wars who offered to attend and who became mentor families to other group members. These factors differentiated it from other Gulf War support groups. Most only targeted spouses, and none opened themselves to this much diversity, including membership covering the life-span.

ENVIRONMENTAL FACTORS

The cooperation between the Red Cross and Family and Children's Service allowed a quick response to the emotional needs of families during an unanticipated crisis. Traditionally, the Red Cross has been well known as a provider of support and comfort to military personnel and their families. Thus, the Red Cross had high credibility as it publicized the support group, and response by military families was immediate. The decision to hold support group meetings in the Red Cross building also facilitated the formation of the group. Family members who might have been uneasy about going to an agency that provided mental health services did feel comfortable going to the Red Cross building. Gulf War support groups that were begun in other kinds of facilities in the Greensboro area, such as a hospital or counseling centers, did not succeed in attracting a viable membership. The strength that Family and Children's Service brought to this group was professional leadership, including the knowledge that a support group must allow expression of feelings rather than just exchange of information.

The location of support group meetings, active publicity efforts by both agencies, and the lack of any screening mechanisms resulted in the timely formation of a large and diverse group. The age range was six months to 68 years. Slightly more than half the members were female. Almost half the members were African-American. The rest were White. The group included two husbands caring for young children following the deployment of wives, the fiancee of a serviceman and her parents, and a grandmother caring for a young child whose parents were both in the Gulf. Most of the wives of the servicemen were employed outside the home but still carried traditional roles in their marriage, so role stress became an important issue for the group. Between 20 and 30 people usually attended, including five to eight children. There was a core group that attended regularly, while others dropped in and out of the group over the course of its 10-month existence. There was a commitment on the part of the agencies and group members to continue the support group as long as the war lasted.

Attention to environmental factors not only helped the group to get started, but also helped the group to continue. Babysitting was provided by high school volunteers, although the decision was soon made to include the children in the adult group for part of the evening. This enriched the group since the children had many feelings to express, similar to the adults. Their inclusion also helped parents understand that children need to express their fears. Some children were also beginning to take on adult roles in these families. Validating this transitional adjustment helped the children feel pride. By having the children in the group, the leaders were able to give the strong message that this should only be a temporary role for the child.

Transportation was a potential problem but arrangements were made for car pooling. The group met in the evening to accommodate members' work schedules. The Red Cross or local service groups provided supper at each meeting, thus removing another potential barrier to attendance.

The war was a stressor that intensely affected the lives of most of the support group members. Older reservists and mothers of young children had been called unexpectedly and with little notice to serve in combat regions. Emotions in the group flared in January when the fighting started and Desert Shield became Desert Storm. The duration of the war and the extent of the danger were unknowns. Families were able to watch the war on television and, as a result, became hypervigilant to a degree that was excessive and damaging. The flood of information seemed to raise anxiety rather than reduce it. Because no one really knew what the media information meant, or what was true, families were confused and often angry without knowing why. Meanwhile, letters from the Gulf were slow to reach families, troops knew little about their destination, and overseas telephone service did not work well. The modern inventions that generally made communication easier did not help families cope with this crisis and sometimes increased stress. Thus, members of the support group tended to have in common intense emotions of anger, fear, confusion, and loneliness.

GROUP COHESIVENESS

The intense shared emotion about a major and uncontrollable world event promoted a strong bond among group members. The diversity of the group also seemed to contribute strongly to group cohesiveness. In addition to differences in gender, race, and age, there were striking differences in socioeconomic status, backgrounds, and political views regarding the war. The group came from a wide geographic area that included rural and urban communities. Not only did group diversity seem to make it easier to welcome new members who joined as time went on, but the group felt and expressed pride in the diversity of its membership. The variety of ages and experiences allowed the group to become a substitute extended family for members living far from their relatives. In fact, this support group carried over beyond planned meetings, as members developed a network of communication and support outside the group as well as during group meetings.

The leaders of this support group used "mutual aid" as the fundamental intervention. Schopler and Galinsky (1993) describe Schwartz's concept of mutual aid as an intervention where group members take "active roles in sharing their experiences, providing information, giving advice, and drawing out other members" (p. 197). Members' differences enriched this process, as people shared different life experiences, perspectives, and coping styles. In an exploratory study of stress reactions among wives of servicemen deployed during the Gulf War, Wexler and McGrath (1991) reported striking differences based on age, ethnicity, and education. Such differences in behavioral attributes perhaps allowed members of this support group to help each other in ways that might not have been possible in a more homogeneous group.

In a discussion of group composition, it is important to note the participation of two couples and several individuals who were veterans of past wars. These members attended not because they had relatives in the Gulf War, but because they saw an opportunity to provide support to families directly affected. These veterans and their spouses shared reassurance about the kind of support available to service personnel in combat areas, information about coping skills developed during lengthy separations, and techniques for coping with post-traumatic stress following the return home. This information helped spouses to maintain hope that their marriage relationships would return to normal after Desert Storm. As group meetings progressed, these veteran families became mentors to other families in the group.

The leaders had three goals in mind when the group began. They wanted to help group members understand that strong emotional reactions were normal; they wanted group members to learn new coping methods to deal with stress; and they wanted to provide a safe place for members to vent anger and other emotions. During initial group meetings, members participated actively in refining group goals. The leaders quickly learned that presentations by guest speakers were not of interest to this group. Members gave the leaders clear feedback that they wanted circle-based discussion of their feelings. There would be no avoidance of their real pain. To encourage normalization and expression of feelings, the group established an introduction ritual that was both formal and informal. Formally, the leaders made sure that new people were introduced and were given information about group norms. Informally, it became a group norm that one had to cry to be a full-fledged member of the group. Almost every new person who joined reported being unable to cry outside the group because most outsiders were not personally affected by the war and did not understand the anguish of families of Desert Storm participants. Such a comment would invariably elicit laughter (supportive, not taunting) and then someone would explain to the new member the informal rule about crying.

Normalization of fear, pain, and isolation brought enormous relief quickly to group members. Learning new coping behaviors was also important. One military wife, for example, reported being unable to sleep in her bed, sleeping instead on the living room floor. She received permission, advice, and support from the group that enabled her to sleep closer to her bed every night. By her third meeting, she announced she was back in her own comfortable bed.

LEADER CHARACTERISTICS

Leader characteristics were important in this group. Both leaders were trained in group dynamics. One was a pastoral counselor and retired Army officer who achieved instant credibility with the group. The co-leader was a clinical social worker. Red Cross personnel participated regularly as technical advisors and hosts. The importance of having trained therapists as co-leaders was brought to the surface during one particularly poignant meeting.

A young woman had joined the group the preceding week, saying nothing at the first meeting but listening attentively and obviously gaining trust. At her second group meeting, she began talking. She spoke in such a halting manner that she took several minutes to complete a few sentences. The story she was telling was filled with sadness. Her husband had had trouble with drinking and had recently tried to stop. She felt that she had not been supportive enough of him before he was called to active duty and sent to the Gulf. She vividly described her feelings of guilt, loneliness, and fear. Before she finished, she stopped for a few seconds and one of the older men, obviously uncomfortable with the halting expression of such intense feelings, spoke out and changed the subject. Others followed and the discussion turned away from her.

The co-leader, recognizing what was happening, brought the group back to this young woman, interpreted the group's sudden shift away from her, and then helped the group to focus on helping her. Almost the entire group was in tears by the time she finished her story. In terms of giving and receiving support, the outcome was positive for her and for the rest of the group. This incident marked a turning point for the group, proving to each member that the group could handle difficult and intense situations. Such trust was important because the potential existed for group members to experience the death of a loved one in the Gulf. In fact, the son of one group member was in a plane shot down during combat but survived the crash.

PROCESS ISSUES AND CLOSURE

The group continued to meet until all relatives were either back home or in a safe environment. Many of the partners, daughters, sons, and other relatives who had been in the Gulf accompanied group members to a final meeting. The leaders found, however, that even though the group had accomplished its stated purpose, several members wished to continue the group. To establish meaning and to permit closure, the leaders asked each participant to express what the group had meant. This exercise helped to bring the group to a successful end.

The reluctance of several group members to terminate led the leaders to consider a possible negative effect of the group. Because the group was so diverse, it included individuals unaccustomed to verbal sharing of intense feelings and support. Although learning to value and practice such skills was generally positive, it may also have been a negative for those who felt bereft of an environment where they could safely continue practicing newly acquired skills.

CONCLUSION

Cooperation between the Red Cross and Family and Children's Service not only promoted the success of this support group but also made it possible for each agency to serve this population of families more effectively. As the group continued, the Red Cross became aware of the needs of individual group members and was able to assist them through Red Cross advocacy services. In turn, two group members became aware of Red Cross needs and became long-term agency volunteers. Approximately 10 group members decided during the course of the support group that they needed therapy and asked the group co-leader for a referral to Family and Children's Service. The honest and open expression encouraged by the group may have helped members make their individual needs known to the Red Cross and to Family and Children's Service. Furthermore, the Red Cross became a portal of entry for such families to get mental health services provided by Family and Children's Service and paid for by the Defense Department.

Collaboration between the two agencies carried over to other crises. After Hurricane Andrew and the California earthquake, the Red Cross provided training, volunteers, material assistance, and transportation, while Family and Children's Service sent professional counselors to assist victims and volunteers. There is now an ongoing relationship between the two agencies, enabling both to deal more quickly and effectively with local emergencies that may arise.

Support groups serve vital functions in communities. Wars, natural disasters, and other events cause distress that can range from mild to serious. Support groups like this one help families to maintain and enhance their strengths. Lessons learned from this support group experience were the importance of sponsorship in providing an appealing environment, the importance of inclusiveness, a greater understanding of the enrichment that diversity brings, and the significance of the role that mentor families can play in a group.

REFERENCES

Kleiger, J.H., Kennedy, D., Becker, D.J., & Smith, S. (1993). "Children, don't forget me": A resource and support group for deployed parents during Operation Desert Shield and Desert Storm. *Health and Social Work*, 18(3), 237-240.

Schopler, J.H., & Galinsky, M.J. (1993). Support groups as open systems: A model for practice and research. *Health and Social Work*, 18(3), 195-207.

Schwartzben, S.H. (1989). The 10th floor family support group: A descriptive model of the use of a multi-family group in a home for the aged. *Social Work with Groups*, 12(1), 41-54.

Stewart, J.B., Hardin, S.B., Weinrich, S., McGeorge, S., Lopez, J., & Pesut, D. (1992). Group protocol to mitigate disaster stress and enhance social support in adolescents exposed to Hurricane Hugo. *Issues in Mental Health Nursing*, 13(2), 105-119.

Wadsworth, R.D. (1993). A Persian Gulf War support group: Process, viability, and flexibility. *International Journal of Group Psychotherapy*, 43(1), 63-76.

Wexler, H.K., & McGrath, E. (1991). Family member stress reactions to military involvement separation. *Psychotherapy*, 28(3), 515-519.

Telephone Support Groups for Caregivers of Persons with AIDS

Andrea Meier
Maeda J. Galinsky
Kathleen A. Rounds

SUMMARY. Caregivers of persons with AIDS experience numerous stressors in their caregiver role and could benefit from support groups. However, caregiving responsibilities make it difficult for many to attend face-to-face groups. This article describes experience with a telephone support group pilot project for this population. The time-limited, semi-structured groups used conference call technology; the eight session group protocol was designed to meet caregiver needs for information about resources and coping skills. Pilot data from interviews with group members from the first two completed groups on this project indicated that participants valued the group experience highly. *[Single or multiple copies of this article are available from The Haworth Document Delivery Service: 1-800-342-678, 9:00 a.m. - 5:00 p.m. (EST).]*

Caring for someone with AIDS can be time-consuming, frustrating, and exhausting. People serving in the caregiver role often find

Andrea Meier, EdM, is a Doctoral Student, Maeda J. Galinsky, PhD, is William R. Kenan Jr. Professor, and Kathleen A. Rounds, PhD, is Associate Professor at the University of North Carolina School of Social Work, 223 East Franklin Street, CB # 3550, Chapel Hill, NC 27599-3550.

The authors wish to thank Patricia Bartlett, Gordon Lipscomb and Martha Zimmerman for their assistance in getting the caregiver groups started and to express appreciation to the caregivers who participated in the groups.

[Haworth co-indexing entry note]: "Telephone Support Groups for Caregivers of Persons with AIDS." Meier, Andrea, Maeda J. Galinsky, and Kathleen A. Rounds. Co-published simultaneously in *Social Work with Groups* (The Haworth Press, Inc.) Vol. 18, No. 1, 1995, pp. 99-108; and: *Support Groups: Current Perspectives on Theory and Practice* (ed: Maeda J. Galinsky, and Janice H. Schopler) The Haworth Press, Inc., 1995, pp. 99-108. Single or multiple copies of this article are available from The Haworth Document Delivery Center [1-800-342-9678, 9:00 a.m. - 5:00 p.m. (EST)].

99

they have neither time nor energy left to satisfy their own needs after meeting the needs of those in their care (Pearlin, 1982; Pilisuk & Parks, 1988; Wardlaw, 1994; Wood, 1994). Innovative services must address caregivers' isolation, constraints on their mobility, and, in the case of AIDS, the stigma associated with caring for someone with this disease. A telephone support group is one relatively new means of intervention, using familiar technology to link caregivers to sources of emotional support and information about resources and ways of effective coping. Conference call technology liberates providers and participants from the logistical limitations of site-specific or regional programs, making social and informational support accessible to homebound, overworked, and/or geographically distant participants (Rittner & Hammons, 1992; Rounds, Galinsky & Stevens, 1991; Wiener, Spencer, Davidson, & Fair, 1993).

The telephone support group project for caregivers of persons with AIDS builds on related telephone groups for persons affected by HIV disease. The caregiver groups are part of our ongoing program to bring supportive social group work services to those who are unable or unwilling to attend face to face groups (Rounds et al., 1991). Following a discussion of the stressors faced by caregivers of persons with AIDS, we present a telephone group pilot project designed for this population and describe our experience with the first two groups.

AIDS CAREGIVER STRESSORS

There has been little systematic study of AIDS caregivers. Research on stressors of people with AIDS and information from practitioners working with families of persons with HIV disease informed the development of the telephone group protocol. Furthermore, since the experience of caregivers of persons with Alzheimer's disease has been well studied and documented, this literature was carefully examined for the insights it could offer in planning group services for caregivers in our project (Toseland, Rossiter, & Labrecque, 1989a; Toseland, Rossiter, & Labrecque, 1989b). Both AIDS and Alzheimer's caregivers must cope with effects of progressive cognitive deterioration and dementia of the people for whom they care.

The following factors were particularly important in the development of the telephone support group protocol for AIDS caregivers. All AIDS caregivers face the daily emotional and physical burdens of caring for a terminally ill person whose symptoms include unpredictable crises and long-term physical and mental deterioration (Kelly & Sykes, 1989). The social stigmatization of HIV disease extends to the family and friends of those who care for an ill person (Rounds et al., 1991). Caregivers' initial reactions to assuming this role (McDonell, Abell, & Miller, 1991; Pearlin, Semple, & Turner, 1988), their access to information, emotional and instrumental support, and their emotional resilience and physical endurance when facing the "imperialism" of the requirements for care (Montgomery, Gonyea, & Hooyman, 1985; Pearlin et al., 1988; Wardlaw, 1994) add varying degrees of stress to their lives. Further, since AIDS is a progressive and terminal disease, unresolved conflicts in the relationship between the caregiver and care receiver, anticipatory bereavement (Murphy & Pearlin, 1988; Pearlin et al., 1988), and planning for matters related to medical and financial decisions and arrangements for burial and remembrance becomes especially important.

The protocol developed for the original telephone support groups for persons who themselves had HIV disease focused on: working with the medical and social care systems; dealing with feelings; telling families and friends about one's involvement with HIV disease; utilizing supportive networks; issues around safe sex; and practical and existential issues related to death and dying (Galinsky, Rounds, Montague, & Butowsky, 1993). Except for the topic of safe sex, these were also important themes in the protocol for caregiver groups but the specific objectives of the sessions and the ways in which these subjects were approached were slanted to the particular needs of caregivers as noted above. Further, attention to taking care of oneself in the face of draining caregiving responsibilities and coping with anticipatory grief were added as subjects to be covered in the group sessions for caregivers.

CAREGIVER TELEPHONE SUPPORT GROUP GOALS AND FORMAT

The telephone support group intervention for caregivers was based on an "open systems model" of groups which emphasized helping participants learn skills to cope with personal and environmental stressors (Schopler & Galinsky, 1993). The intervention consisted of a series of eight, hour-long, semi-structured group sessions that were held via conference calls over the course of ten weeks. The first six sessions were held weekly at regularly scheduled times. The last two sessions took place two weeks apart to enable participants to gradually adjust to the loss of their group's support.

The caregiver telephone support groups were designed to help participants by: (1) providing information about AIDS and community resources; (2) reducing their feelings of isolation related to stigmatization and caregiving role demands; (3) providing a safe environment to express feelings; (4) providing opportunities to reflect on the meaning of losses, and to consider how to confront practical and emotional aspects of death; (5) enhancing interpersonal skills to advocate for care and support; and (6) improving coping and self-care skills to manage stress.

Start-Up Phase

This project was initiated in collaboration with an infectious diseases clinic at a nearby medical center. The participants were recruited by the clinic's social workers. Two groups were planned for this pilot phase of the caregiver support group trials. At the time the groups were being formed, there was a patient cohort of eleven gay men diagnosed with middle or end-stage AIDS, whose mothers were their primary caregivers. Clinic social workers requested that these patients ask their mothers if they were interested in participating in the group; given a positive response, the social workers subsequently spoke to the mother to confirm this interest. Project staff then spoke with the caregivers, explained the evaluation components and obtained their informed consent to participate. Two groups were formed, one of five members, and one of four. Out of the original cohort of eleven mothers two chose not to participate because their sons died prior to the beginning of the groups.

Both leaders were experienced group work practitioners who had previously led telephone groups for persons with HIV disease on the same project. They contacted participants to arrange meeting times, and discussed the need for privacy and uninterrupted use of the telephone for an entire hour during the scheduled group times. Once the groups began, the group leader initiated contact with members each week through conference calls arranged by a telephone conference organization. Participants were given instructions on how to temporarily disable their call waiting services and were provided with the 800 number which would quickly reconnect them with the group if they were disconnected. The conference calls were initiated from the leaders' home phones. Headphones enabled leaders to keep their hands free to take notes. With participants' permission, sessions were also taped for later review by group leaders and project evaluators.

Session Protocol

Each of the first six weekly sessions focused on a specific topic. The final two sessions were left open to address participants' emerging problems and concerns, and to acknowledge their personal growth and successes. Topics were presented in a sequence that allowed participants to develop a sense of safety and confidence in sharing their experiences in a group. In the initial sessions, participants consider how they cope with external stressors; the later sessions provide opportunities for sharing feelings regarding their overwhelming responsibilities, and past, present, and future losses. The general topics and suggested discussion themes for each of the eight sessions are summarized below.

Session 1: Orientation. The group members are introduced to each other. They clarify group norms, and learn about the logistics and processes of telephone support groups. Participants share their expectations about the group, discuss how they became AIDS caregivers, and how their feelings about their caregiving roles have changed over time.

Session 2: Dealing with medical and social services systems. Participants further explore the concept of social support and how the telephone group can be a source of support. Members are invited to share their experiences in trying to obtain information and services from the medical and social services agencies. They discuss, and sometimes role play, behaviors which improve their effectiveness in preventing and coping with problems dealing with medical and social services providers and agencies. Members also discuss legal issues related to HIV disease such as living wills, power of attorney, and estate planning.

Session 3: Maintaining and expanding social support networks. Members discuss problems they have experienced with family, friends, co-workers, and employers as a result of being a caregiver. They consider what may deter them from revealing that they are caring for someone with AIDS, how to decide what to disclose and to whom and, how to ask for help effectively.

Session 4: Coping with stressors of being an AIDS caregiver. Members explore how other parts of their lives have been affected by their roles as caregivers. They also share their reactions about deteriorating physical and mental functioning of the person that they are caring for and reflect on how these changes have affected their relationship with this person. They also receive information about respite care and hospice and discuss how to access these services.

Session 5: Self-care and coping with anticipatory grief, loss, and bereavement. Participants learn about the process of bereavement and share how they cope with feelings of traumatization, loss, and anticipatory grief. Members consider how their feelings of identification with the person for whom they are caring, sense of responsibility for, and helplessness in the face of AIDS can affect their behavior toward this person. Members are encouraged to discuss how they manage the competing demands between their own and the ill person's needs.

Session 6: Review/endings and looking ahead. This session is designed to reinforce and consolidate what members have learned about effective coping and self-care strategies. Participants review ideas raised in the sessions and consider how they will apply them when coping with future situations. They also review how to build and sustain social support networks. They tentatively decide whether to stay in contact with each other and develop guidelines for future contacts. Members explore their feelings about the ending of the group and evaluate the group experience.

Session 7 and 8: Follow-Up (2 and 4 weeks after Session 6). During the two follow-up sessions, members update each other on changes in their situations and explore how these changes have affected them. They discuss emerging issues in their lives, changes in their reactions to current and anticipated losses, and share their problems and successes in their relationships with others, including provider systems. In Session 8, members again review their agreements for staying in contact and discuss their feelings about the final termination of the group.

While there were planned topics for each of the first six sessions, group leaders put aside scheduled topics when members wanted to discuss other more critical issues. In addition, there were contingency plans to contact participants immediately after sessions if they had emotional crises which could not be managed within the group. The leader could then assess the situation and, if necessary, refer them for additional help. In these two groups, the group leaders did not have to contact members outside of the group meeting times.

GROUP EXPERIENCE

As noted earlier, all nine members were mothers of gay males diagnosed with middle or end-stage AIDS. These women ranged in age from 38 years to 73 years with a median age of 58 years. Two were African-American and seven were Caucasian. Five of the women were married, three divorced, and one widowed. Four women had attended or completed college. Three were employed; 4 of the 6 women who were unemployed were disabled. Three of the women reported annual incomes above $30,000, with no one reporting income below $10,000. The median time of active caregiving for their sons was 16 months with a range of 7 months to 60 months. These women also faced other significant challenges in their lives. Several had severe, chronic health problems (e.g., diabetes, glaucoma, severe chronic depression, arthritis, osteoporosis), and were caring for other sick relatives or young children.

We are evaluating the outcomes and the processes of the caregiver telephone support groups through structured pre- and post-intervention questionnaires administered to participants and semi-structured interviews with group leaders. All interviews were conducted on the phone. To monitor session content, practitioners filled out structured written forms after each session and session tapes were transcribed. We are reporting here on preliminary results from post-group participant questionnaires and practitioner interviews for the two groups which we have conducted; a more complete analysis of the data will follow the completion of the project.

Based on a preliminary analysis of data from post-group telephone interviews with group members and leaders, it appears that telephone support groups using this intervention model are well suited to the needs of AIDS caregivers. Participants were unanimously positive in their reactions to the groups. Their comments indicated that they were eager to get as much information as possible about the AIDS-related changes in mental functioning, the implications of various symptoms, the side effects of medication and ways to boost immune function. They reported that the information they received from the group was appropriate, comprehensive, and practical. They particularly appreciated sharing ideas about how to stimulate their son's appetites so they would eat more and slow the wasting process.

Almost everyone reported that talking to people who really understood their problems validated and strengthened their commitment to their caregiving efforts. Some members commented that they used what they learned about assertiveness and limit setting to manage their other family problems as well as conflicts arising specifically from their sons' resistance to their caregiving efforts. In session 2, many members drew on group support for the courage to address the realities of their sons' impending deaths. After discussing the importance of making legal and burial arrangements, several members brought up this concern with their sons and were able to help them make specific arrangements for funerals and burials. The women who did this reported that they felt relieved to have these details finalized.

The group also served as an opportunity to explore the meaning of life and death. In one group, all the members were devoutly religious, but they had been unable to attend church regularly because of caregiving responsibilities and because of their fears of stigmatization. Many of the mothers said that the groups helped them to reconcile themselves to the extreme uncertainty of the near future and the ultimate fact of their sons' deaths. One mother characterized this attitude with the statement: "tomorrow is never given."

Commitment to the groups was very strong. In the post-group

interviews, all participants said that they had looked forward to each session; many felt at loss about what to do with their time when the groups shifted to bi-weekly schedules. Members occasionally missed a session but always returned to the next meeting. Reasons for not attending included the need to be out of town on business, a son's health crisis, and problems with a phone line. All members expressed the desire for more sessions. Members in both groups contracted to stay in touch with each other after the groups ended. When one member's son died two weeks after the final session, she notified all the members of the group and two of the members attended the funeral.

All of the participants reported that they felt comfortable with the conference call format; several mentioned that, by *not* meeting face-to-face, it was easier to express their feelings. All of the women were strained by the logistical problems of trying to care for their sons and insure that they received adequate treatment, so they appreciated the convenience of participating in the group from home.

Outcome data on the small sample presented here are a preliminary step in the evaluation of the telephone groups for AIDS caregivers. Further study of the data with a larger sample should give us a more complete picture of the group processes and outcomes, including benefits and limitations. However, what seems clear from these preliminary results is that using conference call technology appears to be a viable way to provide support and information. It seems particularly helpful in improving access to support groups for an overburdened population such as caregivers of persons with AIDS. Although the groups were time-limited, participants' reports about their experiences in the group indicated that access to information and support helped them cope with a wide range of stressors.

REFERENCES

Galinsky, M., Rounds, K., Montague, A., & Butowsky, E. (1993). *Leading a telephone support group for persons with HIV disease: A training manual for group leaders.* Chapel Hill, NC: School of Social Work, University of North Carolina at Chapel Hill.

Kelly, J., & Sykes, P. (1989). Helping the helpers: A support group for family members of persons with AIDS. *Social Work, 34*(3), 239-242.

McDonell, J. R., Abell, N., & Miller, J. (1991). Family member's willingness to care for people with AIDS: A psychosocial assessment model. *Social Work, 36*(1), 43-53.

Montgomery, R. J., Gonyea, J. G., & Hooyman, N. R. (1985). Caregiving and the experience of subjective and objective burden. *Family Relations, 34*, 19-26.

Murphy, P., & Perry, K. (1988). Hidden grievers. *Death Studies, 12,* 451-462.

Pearlin, L. I. (1982). The social contexts of stress. In L. Goldberger & S. Breznitz (Eds.), *Handbook of stress: Theoretical and clinical aspects* (pp. 367-379). New York: The Free Press.

Pearlin, L. I., Semple, S., & Turner, H. (1988). Stress of AIDS caregiving: A preliminary overview of the issues. *Death Studies, 12,* 501-517.

Pilisuk, M., & Parks, S. H. (1988). Caregiving: Where families need help. *Social Work, 33*(5), 436-440.

Rittner, B., & Hammonds, K. (1993). Telephone group work with people with end stage AIDS. *Social Work with Groups, 15*(4), 59-72.

Rounds, K. A., Galinsky, M. J., & Stevens, L. S. (1991). Linking people with AIDS in rural communities: The telephone group. *Social Work, 36*(1), 13-22.

Schopler, J. H., & Galinsky, M. J. (1993). Support groups as open systems: A model for practice and research. *Health and Social Work, 18*(3), 195-207.

Toseland, R.W., Rossiter, C.M., & Labrecque, M.S. (1989a). The effectiveness of peer-led and professionally led groups to support family caregivers. *The Gerontologist, 29*(4), 465-471.

Toseland, R.W., Rossiter, C.M., & Labrecque, M.S. (1989b). Group interventions to support family caregivers: A review and analysis. *The Gerontologist, 29*(4), 438-448.

Wardlaw, L. A. (1994). Sustaining informal caregivers for persons with AIDS. *Families in Society, 75*(6), 373-384.

Wiener, L.S., Spencer, E.D., Davidson, C., & Fair, C. (1993). National telephone support groups: A new avenue toward psychosocial support for HIV-infected children and their families. *Social Work with Groups, 16*(3), 55-71.

Wood, J. T. (1994). *Who cares?: Women, care, and culture*. Carbondale IL: Southern Illinois University Press.

Computer-Based Self-Help Groups: A New Resource to Supplement Support Groups

Jerry Finn

SUMMARY. Computer-based self-help groups utilize existing tele-communication networks to provide information and support for a variety of social problems. This article discusses their use as an adjunct to support groups. Computer-based groups offer advantages including elimination of time and distance barriers, lack of group size restrictions, increased variety and diversity of support, anonymity, pre- and post-group support, opportunity for expression through written communication, and potential training experiences for group leaders. A pilot project using a computer-based group for sexual abuse survivors is described, and the need for research related to process and outcome in computer-based groups. *[Single or multiple copies of this article are available from The Haworth Document Delivery Service: 1-800-342-9678, 9:00 a.m. - 5:00 p.m. (EST).]*

The use of computer-based self-help/mutual aid groups is an important recent development in providing support to thousands of people with a variety of human service-related concerns including physical and sexual abuse, addictions, AIDS, disability, catastrophic illness, mental illness, and care-giving. These groups are similar in philosophy and intervention techniques to face-to-face support and

Jerry Finn, PhD, is Associate Professor and Chair, Department of Social Work, Arizona State University West, P.O. Box 37100, Phoenix, AZ 85069-7100.

[Haworth co-indexing entry note]: "Computer-Based Self-Help Groups: A New Resource to Supplement Support Groups." Finn, Jerry. Co-published simultaneously in *Social Work with Groups* (The Haworth Press, Inc.) Vol. 18, No. 1, 1995, pp. 109-117; and: *Support Groups: Current Perspectives on Theory and Practice* (ed: Maeda J. Galinsky, and Janice H. Schopler) The Haworth Press, Inc., 1995, pp. 109-117. Single or multiple copies of this article are available from The Haworth Document Delivery Center [1-800-342- 9678, 9:00 a.m. - 5:00 p.m. (EST)].

109

self-help groups, but take place without the constraints of time and distance by utilizing existing telecommunication networks as "meeting places." Computer-based self-help groups are a resource which is only beginning to be discovered by group work professionals.

Support groups, when viewed from an ecological perspective and an open systems model, must take into account other helping modalities in the community. Given the similarity of goals and focus, self-help groups can be seen as a possible adjunct to support group services. Computer-based self-help groups may be useful in providing additional support and information to support group members, especially to those with high needs for support, interpersonal difficulties, and/or esoteric concerns beyond the group's central concerns. Although references to the existence of computer-based self-help groups have been limited, a number of authors describe the promise of the computer to promote greater relatedness among members of society by reducing barriers of time, distance and social status through the formation of "electronic" or "virtual communities" (Marciuskszo, 1990; Furlong, 1989; Naisbit, 1982; Vallee, 1982). The rapid growth of computer communications has provided the vehicle for an extensive network of computer-based self-help/mutual aid groups. Computer-based groups utilize commercial information utilities such as CompuServe (*PC Magazine*, 1991), the Internet system (Kroll, 1992) which links the nation's universities, and private computer based bulletin board systems (Johnson, 1987). There are anecdotal descriptions of individuals being helped through such groups (Madera, 1989; *Newsweek*, 1989; Scott, 1988); descriptions of the structure and extent of participation in public and commercial computer-based self-help groups; and profiles of specific computer-based self-help groups for addictions and survivors of sexual abuse (Finn and Lavitt, 1994; Finn, 1994; Finn, 1993; Sparks, 1992; Madera, 1991). Many of the therapeutic elements of in-person groups, such as support, information, problem solving, diminishment of shame and guilt, and acknowledgment of the universality of experience are present in the electronic medium, and for many members, computer-based self-help groups provide satisfying and long term support (Finn and Lavitt, 1994).

It is not uncommon for members of one helping modality to

participate in another. In some cases, membership in one type of group (e.g., support) leads to information and support which prompts membership in another group (e.g., treatment). In other cases, support and self-help/mutual aid groups have been used as a transition from treatment groups, providing on-going support and follow-up to group treatment. In still other instances, members may belong to more than one type of group simultaneously. Leaders may formally help to make the transition to other groups or the process may happen more informally and circumstantially. The same may be said of computer-based self-help groups, although there has been no study of the extent to which members of computer-based self-help groups participate in other in-person helping processes. *Newsweek* (1989) reported the story of a woman who participated for many weeks on a Recovery (alcohol related) bulletin board system and eventually was able to attend an in-person AA meeting as a result of support and friendships made on the computer-based self-help group. In addition, in this author's reading of several thousand e-mail messages from Sexual Abuse Survivors and Recovery bulletin board systems conferences, many participants spontaneously acknowledge belonging to in-person support and treatment groups. Although computer-based self-help members participate in other in-person groups, there have been no reports of support or treatment groups facilitating linkage with computer-based self-help groups.

THE UTILITY OF COMPUTER-BASED SELF-HELP GROUPS

Computer-based self-help groups "meet" through "echo conferences." Echo conferences are topic specific, and are the medium through which computer based self-help is transmitted. Members generally do not correspond with each other in "real time." Members post messages on a conference in a manner similar to electronic mail in the business sector. Messages may be addressed to specific individuals or may be addressed to "ALL"; however, messages are available for all members to read in a manner analogous to a bulletin board in a public place. Members may read mail and post messages while logged on to the conference. Members, however, often have software that allows them to automate the process of receiving (downloading) their messages. The software also permits them to answer their mail "off-line" and later send replies in-batch (all at once) to the conference. Some members download the entire conference while others automate receiving mail addressed specifically to themselves. Each conference has a moderator who monitors discussion to keep it civil and topic focused. (Moderators are generally nonprofessional experienced group members who volunteer for the position. In some cases they are self-appointed originators of the group; in other cases group members vote on who will be the moderator when the position is open). Everyday the sysop (system operator) uploads the latest messages to a regional hub and downloads any new messages from the hub. Once a day, the regional hub calls the national hub and makes its own up/downloads. The result is that messages are usually posted on all systems which carry the conference within two days.

Linking support group members with computer-based self-help groups has a number of theoretical and practical advantages. First, computer-based self-help groups can provide supplemental support for members when face-to-face groups are not available. This is especially useful for members who require a great deal of support. Computer-based self-help groups help to diffuse dependency needs across a larger population. Participation barriers related to time and distance are eliminated. If members have home computers, computer-based self-help groups are available on a 24 hour basis. If computers are made available at the sponsoring organization, they can be used independently by members whenever the organization is open. Finn and Lavitt (1994) report members using computer-based self-help groups from home during early morning hours and when too ill to attend a face-to-face group.

Computer-based self-help groups offer a greater degree of anonymity than face-to-face groups. Using pseudonyms, members place and receive messages without cues related to age, sex, race, and physical appearance. This allows some members, especially in groups dealing with stigmatized issues such as sexual abuse, to more easily and safely begin to explore sensitive issues. Members with interpersonal or communication difficulties may also find sharing information in written form a safe way to begin to explore personal issues. This may facilitate members in later dealings with these issues in the support group.

Another potential advantage of linkage with computer-based self-help groups is the greater number of participants from which information and perspectives may be drawn. Some computer-based self-help groups have several hundred members throughout the United States and Canada. One member of a computer-based self-help group for physically disabled people asked about summer camps for disabled preadolescent girls. Another member from a distant state provided a file containing a list of such camps throughout the United States. Information gained on computer-based self-help groups can be shared in the face-to-face group.

Computer-based self-help groups may also prove to be useful when there are too few or too many members for optimum group conditions. Computer-based self-help groups could be used during a wait list period to provide support to potential members until in-person support group resources are available. Or, in the case of new groups in which there may be only a few members in the formative period of the group, computer-based self-help groups could provide a supplemental source of support and information for members.

The use of journals, stories, and poetry has been an effective tool for promoting recovery for many social problems, especially in areas related to physical and sexual abuse (Dinsmore, 1991). Computer-based self-help groups provide members an opportunity to share journal entries, poetry, and other art such as drawings with a wide audience. These avenues of emotional expression can provide a supplement to in-person support group processes.

Finally, computer-based self-help groups can provide an additional source of training for new support group leaders. Leadership in support groups in based primarily on skills in group facilitation rather than personal experience with the focal group problem. Participation in a computer-based self-help group provides potential leaders with the thoughts, feelings and issues surrounding a specific problem, promoting both knowledge and empathy. For example, a leader might participate in a computer-based self-help group for members with Multiple Personality Disorder (MPD) in order to gain insight and knowledge regarding this problem. Such knowledge would be an excellent supplement for leaders of in-person sexual abuse survivors groups since it is possible that some members of their own groups may have these difficulties.

ASU WEST PILOT PROJECT

A computer-based self-help group is being used in a pilot project as an adjunct to a support group for sexual abuse survivors at the ASU West Women's Resource Center. Students in an on-going support group are told about the computer-based group and are shown a demonstration session. The computer-based group is presented as an opportunity to share experiences with a wide range of people throughout the country. The goals of providing computer-based self-help are to: provide greater access to additional support; increase members sense of universality; provide greater opportunities for therapeutic behaviors such as self-revealing, taking the role of helper, and problem solving; diffuse dependency on the current support group; and provide follow-up support at the end of the support group. Thus far, only two women have utilized this service, but six others have indicated interest in this resource and will participate next semester after they have been trained in using the computer-based self-help group. The two students using the system were already computer literate and needed about half an hour training in accessing the computer-based self-help group. It is estimated that less computer literate students will require about two hours of training with some additional on-going technical support.

Students are able to access *Alt.Sex.Abuse.Recovery,* a computer-based self-help group on the Internet. This Internet-based group carries several hundred messages each week from participants across the United States and from some foreign countries. It is available through most colleges and universities as well as through some commercial services. Students have access to their computer-based self-help group through two computers located in the Womens Resource Center or through the student computing facility. Students can access the group anytime during normal university hours. In addition, students with a home computer and modem can access the group on a twenty-four hour basis.

The Internet is not a particularly user-friendly system; after the initial learning phase, however, students were able to use the group with relative ease. Students establish anonymous identities on the computer-based group, and participate about twice a week for approximately one half hour each session. No formal attempt is made to integrate the support group with the computer-based self-help group. The students initial reaction to the computer-based group, based on four weeks of participation, has been mixed.

One student found the group particularly useful. In an open-ended interview she stated that she believed that some members of the computer-based group had a greater understanding of her issues than the face-to-face support group. In part, the lack of face-to-face contact facilitated her willingness to discuss memories of past sexual abuse. She was able to share some experiences on the computer-based group that she would not be willing to discuss in her support group. She plans to continue using the computer-based group after the support group ends.

The other student stated that she found the computer-based group "interesting" because of the wide variety of experiences, but that she preferred the face-to-face group. While she read many messages, she rarely posted her own messages. She stopped using the computer-based group after the third week, stating that she did not have time to spend on the group. It is impossible to draw any conclusions based on the limited experience of two participants. It is likely that, as with many different kinds of support, computer-based groups will work well for some people and will be less useful for others. The experience of these two students underscores the need for much continued research to determine the usefulness of computer-base self-help groups and for whom the groups are most appropriate.

Following this exploratory research, more extensive and controlled studies need to be conducted in order to determine the value and utility of computer-based self-help groups as well as to examine potential harm or problems associated with their use. Since this is a new area, exploratory research using extensive open-ended interviews needs to be conducted. Members' experiences must be evaluated to answer a number of research questions related to both process and outcome. How often and for how long do members participate in the computer-based self-help groups? What is the impact of different formats? What is the nature of group interaction on the computer-based group? What is the extent of participation, and how do people decide with whom and how often to interact? What are the perceived benefits and the perceived negative consequences to participation? To what extent are relationships formed on computer-based self-help groups? How do participation patterns for in-person and computer-based self-help groups compare? What is the interaction of in-person and computer-based self-help groups? For example, do members bring issues and information from computer-based self-help groups into the in-person group for discussion? Conversely, do members continue to process their in-person group participation in the computer-based self-help group? If so, is the effect synergistic or diluting? Support group leaders should also be asked for their perceptions of these issues.

CONCLUSION

Theoretically, computer-based self-help groups offer tremendous potential to provide information and support to people with the very concerns currently addressed by the support groups. Given the limited number of trained leaders, computer-based self-help groups could provide an important adjunct to in-person support groups as part of a wait list condition, as a source of concurrent support, and as follow up support to time limited groups. Many computer-based self-help groups already exist through computer BBS conferences and through the Internet, and thousands of people are already utilizing them. Thus far, there has been little systematic evaluation of computer-based self-help groups and no research about their use as an adjunct to in-person support groups. This is a new practice and research area for the professional support group community and there is much work to be done.

REFERENCES

Dinsmore, C. (1991). *From surviving to thriving: Incest, feminism and recovery.* Albany: State University of New York Press.

Finn, J. (In Press). "Computer-based self-help groups: On-line recovery for addictions." *Computers in Human Services* 12 (3).

Finn, J. (1993). An exploration of computer-based self-help/mutual aid groups. In B. Glastonbury, (Ed.) *Human welfare and technology: Papers from the HUSITA 3 conference.* (pp. 70-79) Assen: Van Gorcum.

Finn, J. and M. Lavitt (1994). "Computer-based self-help/mutual aid groups for sexual abuse survivors." *Social Work with Groups,* 17(1/2), pp. 21-46.

Furlong, Mary S. (1989). An electronic community for older adults: The senior network; *Journal of Communication, 39* (3), 145-153.

Johnson, S. (1987). Nonprofit and public service telecomputing. Paper presented at the First International Human Service Information Technology Applications Conference, Birmingham, England, September.

Madera, E.J. (1991). Mutual aid self-help on-line: The new telecommunities. Paper presented at the International Conference on Computer Technology and Human Services in the 90's: HUSITA 2, Rutgers University, NJ. September.

Maciuszko, K.L. (1990). A quiet revolution: community online systems, *Online, 14* (6), pp. 24-32.

Naisbitt, J. (1982). *Megatrends.* New York: Warner Books.

Newsweek (1989). Very personal computing, Aug. 28. p. 14.

PC Magazine (November 12, 1991). After hours, fun and fulfillment at 2400 bps: The personal side of on-line services, pp. 53-56.

Sparks, S. M. (1992). Exploring electronic support groups, *American Journal of Nursing, 12,* pp. 62-65.

Vallee, J. (1982). *The network revolution: Confessions of a computer scientist.* Berkeley: And/Or Press.

Index

Acquired immune deficiency syndrome patients, caregivers for. *See* People with AIDS caregivers

Advocacy groups, for caregivers of frail older adults, 18-19,22

Advocates, for support group programs, 69

African-Americans, support group membership of
in Grandmothers as Mothers Again, 70
in male partners of sexual abuse survivors groups, 84
in military family groups, 91
in people with AIDS caregiver groups, 105
in sickle cell disease mutual assistance groups, 8,55-65

Agencies, support groups' integration with, 68-69,76,77

AIDS patients, caregivers. *See* People with AIDS caregivers

Alzheimer's disease patients, caregivers for, 21,100

Anxiety, postpartum, 42,43

Arizona State University West Women's Resource Center, sexual abuse survivors support group project of, 114-116

Baby blues, 43,51

Bereavement, of caregivers for people with AIDS, 104,107

Bereavement groups, for relatives and spouses of cancer patients, 29,30, 32,33,36

Bradburn Affect Balance Scale, 21

Brief Symptom Inventory, 21,27,31, 33-34,35-36,38

Brookdale Grandparent Caregiver Information Project, 72

Bulletin board services, computer-based, 110,111,116

Burnout, of support group leaders, 7

Cancer Care, Inc., 29-39

Cancer support groups, 8,27-40
community-based programs, 27-40
bereavement groups, 29,30,32, 33,36
Brief Symptom Inventory data, 27,31,33-34,35-36,38
Cancer Care, Inc. program, 29-39
evaluation of, 30-39
Group Evaluation Questionnaire for, 31,33, 34-35,38
group bonds in, 36-37
group facilitators of, 29-30,33, 38
patients' support groups, 29, 30,32,33,36
psychoeducational groups, 27-28
effect on psychological distress, 33-34,35-36,37-38
recommendations for, 37, 38-39
relatives' support groups, 29, 30,32
supportive-expressive approach of, 29-30

Haworth
DOCUMENT DELIVERY
SERVICE

This valuable service provides a single-article order form for any article from a Haworth journal.

- *Time Saving:* No running around from library to library to find a specific article.
- *Cost Effective:* All costs are kept down to a minimum.
- *Fast Delivery:* Choose from several options, including same-day FAX.
- *No Copyright Hassles:* You will be supplied by the original publisher.
- *Easy Payment:* Choose from several easy payment methods.

Open Accounts Welcome for ...
- Library Interlibrary Loan Departments
- Library Network/Consortia Wishing to Provide Single-Article Services
- Indexing/Abstracting Services with Single Article Provision Services
- Document Provision Brokers and Freelance Information Service Providers

---

MAIL or *FAX* THIS ENTIRE ORDER FORM TO:

Haworth Document Delivery Service
The Haworth Press, Inc.
10 Alice Street
Binghamton, NY 13904-1580

or FAX: 1-800-895-0582
or CALL: 1-800-342-9678
9am-5pm EST

PLEASE SEND ME PHOTOCOPIES OF THE FOLLOWING SINGLE ARTICLES:

1) Journal Title: _____
   Vol/Issue/Year: _____ Starting & Ending Pages: _____
   Article Title: _____
   _____

2) Journal Title: _____
   Vol/Issue/Year: _____ Starting & Ending Pages: _____
   Article Title: _____
   _____

3) Journal Title: _____
   Vol/Issue/Year: _____ Starting & Ending Pages: _____
   Article Title: _____
   _____

4) Journal Title: _____
   Vol/Issue/Year: _____ Starting & Ending Pages: _____
   Article Title: _____
   _____

(See other side for Costs and Payment Information)

COSTS: Please figure your cost to order quality copies of an article.

1. Set-up charge per article: $8.00
    ($8.00 × number of separate articles) _____

2. Photocopying charge for each article:

    1-10 pages: $1.00 _____

    11-19 pages: $3.00 _____

    20-29 pages: $5.00 _____

    30+ pages: $2.00/10 pages _____

3. Flexicover (optional): $2.00/article _____

4. Postage & Handling: US: $1.00 for the first article/
    $.50 each additional article _____

    Federal Express: $25.00 _____

    Outside US: $2.00 for first article/
    $.50 each additional article _____

5. Same-day FAX service: $.35 per page _____

GRAND TOTAL: _____

METHOD OF PAYMENT: (please check one)

❑ Check enclosed   ❑ Please ship and bill. PO # _____
    (sorry we can ship and bill to bookstores only! All others must pre-pay)

❑ Charge to my credit card: ❑ Visa;   ❑ MasterCard;   ❑ Discover;
    ❑ American Express;

Account Number:_____ Expiration date:_____

Signature: ✗_____

Name: _____ Institution: _____

Address: _____

_____

City: _____ State:_____ Zip:_____

Phone Number: _____ FAX Number: _____

MAIL or *FAX* THIS ENTIRE ORDER FORM TO:

Haworth Document Delivery Service | **or FAX:** 1-800-895-0582
The Haworth Press, Inc. | **or CALL:** 1-800-342-9678
10 Alice Street | 9am-5pm EST)
Binghamton, NY 13904-1580 |